The Yielding is a beautiful classic of Christian devotion, allied with a modern voice and personal testimonies, from the authors' own lives. The Body of Christ needs voices like them that call believers beyond the self-help style "Christian Lite" thinking into real maturity and fullness. I heartily recommend this book by my friends, Kathi and Jeffrey Pelton, to everyone who wants to experience all the benefits of the ministry of the life of Jesus Christ today.

Joan Hunter
Author/Evangelist
www.joanhunter.org

Honestly, this book had me at the title, and it only continued from there. Jeffrey and Kathi Pelton have offered a beautiful, deep, personal invitation into the too often misunderstood joy of yielding and surrender to the Lover of Our Souls. They have put their hearts, wisdom and their process on paper so that we the reader can be welcomed into their lives, community, and even more, they welcome us into the Father's embrace for the great transformation to take place in, and through, our lives.

The Yielding is an open door for you to partake of the fullness of God, while diving deeper into what will become an unyielding fullness in your heart as well. Most of all, you're being led on this journey by a trusted source—not just by those who have walked it out, but by those who have obviously allowed this surrendered life to have its full course within them.

Joey LeTourneau
www.ifgodhadahouse.com

The Yielding is a road map for the heart in the pursuit of intimacy. It inspires, compels and inflames fresh surrender to the one your heart longs for. Writing a book about yieldedness to God requires hearts that are particularly yielded. Jeffrey and Kathi Pelton certainly have such hearts and have long walked the walk and lived their lives as laid-down lovers. We believe that in reading this book you will both encounter Holy Spirit in a fresh way and hunger for more than ever before.

Ben & Jodie Hughes
Pour it Out Ministries
www.pouritout.org

The
Yielding

The Yielding

A Lifestyle of Surrender

Jeffrey and Kathi Pelton

The Yielding

Published by Inscribe Press
Tigard, OR

Cover design by Pelton Media Group, Horseheads, NY

ISBN 978-1-7327707-0-6

10 9 8 7 6 5 4 3 2 1

INSCRIBE

Dedication

To David and Ruth Demian and the global family of Watchmen for the Nations, who have taught us how to walk in the beauty of a yielded lifestyle. Your sacrifice and surrender is a fragrance unto the King that is restoring His original intent among the nations and answering the prayer of Jesus in John 17. We love you all. Our Lord will receive His full inheritance!

Contents

Acknowledgments

Foreword by Daneen Bottler 1

Foreword by David Demian 3

Introduction 5

Prologue: A Vision in the Night 15

Section One: Freed from Accusation and the Land of Bondage

1. Beginnings 19
2. The Gift of Vulnerability 23
3. Let Go and Let God 27
4. You are the Apple of God's Eye 31

Selah—When the Father Held My Hair Back (Kathi Pelton) 35

5. The LORD Fights for You 37
6. Not By Might... 41
7. From Regret to Restoration 45
8. You Will Be Transformed 49

Selah—Breakthrough for Malaysia (Marilyn Ongkili) 53

Section Two: He Does What We Cannot

9. Star of Wonder 59
10. Our Lives Declare His Glory 63
11. You are of Great Value 67

12. Receiving Wisdom 71

Selah—Our "Yes" to God (Ty Bottler) 75

13. The Sound of His Answer 77

14. I Will Not Fear 83

15. Peace on Earth, Goodwill to Men 87

16. The God of Second Chances 91

Selah—Yielding to His Spirit (Jodie Hughes) 95

<u>Section Three</u>: Clothed in New Garments

17. Grace Sufficient 103

18. God Purifies what the Enemy has Defiled 107

19. Clothed in Fine White Linen 111

20. You Will See Clearly 115

Selah—Confronting a Python Spirit (Garris Elkins) 117

21. God Reunites what was Divided 121

22. Rushing Wind 125

23. Watch as God Vindicates You 129

24. Stand Firm! Your Victory Comes From the LORD 133

Selah—Standing Firm (An interview with Steve Trujillo) 137

<u>Section Four</u>: Rejoicing and Walking in the "New"

25. It's Time for Abundant Life 145

26. He Grants True Wisdom 147

27. Intentional Surrender 151

28. The Blank Check ("If You...) 155

Selah—The Surprises of Yielding (Peter Jordan) 159

29. God Grants the Desires of Your Heart 163

30. Light Shines in the Darkness 167

31. A New Script Inscribed on Your Life 171

32. One Spirit with Christ 175

Section Five: Preparing for the "Greater Things" (What Happened Before Will Happen Again!)

33. He Gives us Pure Oil 181

34. Lost Things Suddenly Found 185

35. Miracles That Happened Before Will Happen Again 189

36. Do Not Fret...Trust Him 193

37. In a Single Day, Everything Can Change 197

Selah—The Other Side of Yes (Ben Hughes) 201

38. Beyond Fantasy 205

39. The Fierce Love of Our Bridegroom 209

40. It is Finished 213

Epilogue: Consummation 217

Works Cited 219
Contributor Biographies 221
About the Authors 225

Acknowledgments

Just as "no man is an island," so no book springs entire from an unaided individual. There are many people besides the authors without whom this book would not exist.

We wrote most of the original devotions while on the road and were honored and privileged to stay with Gene and Sandy Heacock in their amazing "house of prayer on the rock" in Gloucester, MA overlooking Boston.

Brad and Jodi Bodenman graciously turned over their awesome house on the water in Gig Harbor, WA for us to write the initial drafts for the book.

Daneen Bottler gave us many vital insights and prophetic words, and provided the book's subtitle when we just couldn't seem to come up with something we both liked! She also did a marvelous foreword.

The people at Father's House City Ministries provided encouragement, prayer, family, and support. They are a people and a house like no other!

Gerry and Aurora Presley gave us friendship and love (and a wonderful garden to sit in) in Santa Rosa, CA as we completed the finishing touches editing and formatting the book, and sowed generously into practical needs of Inscribe Publishing.

Our son Corey, the head of Pelton Media Group in upstate New York, is energetic and creative, and he has a fantastic ability to take our cover ideas and create art! Also thanks to Corey and Brittany for making three of the most adorable grandsons ever to visit the planet.

Ty Bottler, Garris Elkins, Ben and Jodie Hughes, Peter Jordan, Marilyn Ongkili, and Steve Trujillo were selfless in their willingness to share their stories and be transparent with us. They are all sterling examples of devotion to the Kingdom of God.

And a special thanks to our adult children and their spouses, who have embraced their parents' yielded—and at times crazy—lifestyle! Desiree', Corey, Brittany, Luke, Amy, and Jonathan—we love and honor you. Your vibrancy and joy inspires us, you fill our days to overflowing with beauty and laughter, and we truly can't imagine our lives without you.

Foreword

The Lord is looking for a people who will volunteer in the day of His power. A people who will partner with Him to demonstrate the knowledge, the intimate knowing of His glory (His character, His nature, His majesty), in the earth today. Who is it that is being called to volunteer in the day of His power? Who is it that is being called to rise up and incarnate Christ to the world around us? We, the children of God are being called in this season and this very hour, to display to the world around us God's glory and His power!

As believers, we can easily become comfortable and acclimated to being in a revival service and atmosphere; a place where hearts are awakened from their slumber to the reality of the presence of God, through the Holy Spirit. As good as revival meetings and conferences are, they will not bring lasting transformation or reformation to the world around us. Romans chapter eight tells us that "All of creation is groaning," waiting "with eager expectation for the sons of God to be revealed." The prophet Habakkuk boldly declares in Habakkuk 2:14,
"The earth will be filled with the knowledge of the glory of the Lord, as waters cover the sea."

But how is this knowledge of His glory to come about? When will the sons and daughters of God be revealed? The filling of the earth with the knowledge of the glory of God happens as the sons and daughters of God themselves become yielded vessels, allowing themselves first to be shaped and formed by His glory in order to release it to the world around them.

It is only when we willingly yield our self-will and lay our lives down on the altar, and we surrender our hearts and ways to be shaped and formed by God's heart and ways, that we become transformed into His image-bearers, displaying to the world the image of the Father's Beloved Son, the Lord Jesus Christ. It is only in the posture of yielding to the Holy Spirit that our lives become consecrated vessels of honor for the Lord to pour His glory into. This must be our heart's cry and longing in every moment and in every breath we breathe. As we yield to His leading, as we obey His voice and surrender ourselves fully to His making, the Lord comes and fills us to overflowing with His glory. We then begin, out of our inmost being, to release the knowledge of the fullness of Him, effectively transforming and reforming the world around us. In essence, as we are yielded fully to the Lord, we become agents of transformation, establishing His Kingdom and releasing an awareness and demonstration of His glory everywhere we go. This is why Jeffrey and Kathi Pelton's book *The Yielding* is such a vital and important book for the body of Christ today.

Jeff and Kathi have beautifully written a book that offers those that read it an intimate invitation into "oneness" with Christ and challenges them to not only volunteer in the day of His power, but to posture themselves into a lifestyle of being consecrated and yielded vessels, that the Lord can continually pour His glory through. As you read through the pages of this life changing book, you will encounter testimonies of God's goodness in the midst of yielding. The Great Shepherd is calling your name inviting you into the depths of His heart and to a place of yielding to His love in a deeper way. Transformation and reformation always begin with a yielded heart that says: "Be it unto me, according to your word."

Daneen Bottler
Ty and Daneen Bottler Ministries
www.tyanddaneenbottler.com

Foreword

Jeff and Kathi Pelton invite us through this book on a personal as well as global family journey—a journey of yielding, surrendering, and submitting to the Lord. A journey of continuing consecration, of being cleansed and purified. A journey of aligning to be one spirit with the Lord. Hear the Spirit of the Lord calling us to go deeper and come up higher into the presence of the Lord. Prepare for the season of the revealing of the sons of God!

We were all deeply touched and transformed last year when Jeff and Kathi wrote the daily life-changing articles during the "Yielding." Many throughout the world followed them and commented on them.

Now the Peltons have developed these insights into a beautiful book that will touch many more. I am praying that this will be released into the nations and will also be a blessing to them to see how many lives are changed.

We love them and honor them.

David Demian
Watchmen for the Nations
https://watchmen.org

Introduction

The body of Christ is at the threshold of an historic, world-wide outpouring of the presence of God and the power of the Holy Spirit such as we have never known. This has been prophesied through the millennia since the time of the early church fathers and has been a hope and expectation of all generations of believers. As millions have gone on to become part of the great cloud of witnesses, we sense the groaning, as well as the excitement, of the Holy Spirit drawing us into fervent prayer and intercession, releasing the family call of the redeemed: "Abba, Father!" and stirring our hearts into the longing cry of the bride: "Come, Lord Jesus!"

The spirit of prayer has gained momentum through the centuries, causing an ever-growing, ever-expanding work of faith in God's people to understand that the kingdoms of this world have become the kingdoms of our Lord and of His Messiah. Now more than ever, we realize that we are in the last days of the history of our planet; as a global people, we have sensed that we are in a season of acceleration. The entire body of Jesus—both Jews who have come to know their Messiah, and Gentiles who have been grafted in—realize that the glorious time of Jesus' appearing, and His ultimate defeat of every foe, is at hand, at out very door.

Our adversary, satan, knows this as well; he realized his time is short, and because of this, he is frightened and greatly enraged. He has never ceased his assaults on humanity in his desire to steal, kill, and destroy; he have never ceased in his campaign to deceive the gullible and malign the faithful.

In the book of Zechariah, chapter three, we read the account of the accuser standing next to Joshua the high priest, in the presence of Almighty

God. As *kohen gadol,* high priest of Israel, Joshua represents not only an individual, but he also stands as representative of a people group; and since that group is the nation of Israel, chosen to be a blessing to all nations of the earth, it can be said that he represents all humanity, in our brokenness and failure.

Joshua stands before the holy one, guilty and covered in shame, wearing garments soiled with sin. Satan gleefully accuses Joshua, pointing out his wickedness and by extension, the wickedness and failure of all people for all time. He also uses the opportunity to accuse God, for the enemy longs to find fault with the Almighty and point out, if it is possible, how His plans and purposes for the people He loves have failed and continue to fail. Our accuser ultimately lays the responsibility of our failures at the feet of our eternal Creator and uses that as an occasion to accuse God Himself.

In this day, many of us who belong to the Lord have felt the dreadful coldness of accusation against us, as we become aware of our failures and sin and the sins of our nations. Because we have often been unfaithful as a people, so satan desires to taunt the very goodness of God and accuse Him of unfaithfulness as well. When we find ourselves disappointed, we can sometimes become discouraged and even angry, and with our hearts weakened by our failure and the disappointment of circumstances, we become susceptible to the lies of the enemy of our souls. This causes more failure and gives additional ammunition to satan to continue his relentless recitation of lies and recriminations.

But God in His mercy, goodness, and authority, rebukes the very taunts of the enemy and throws them back into his face. He declares Himself as the one who has chosen Jerusalem; He is the one who has determined that He will place His presence there to remain with us, creating us fully as His people and drawing all who are thirsty to come and drink the living water of life. He has chosen us as His people, His very beloved, and just like Joshua, we are brands plucked from the fires of our own foolishness and the selfishness of our catastrophically broken world.

> *Then he showed me Joshua the high priest standing before the angel of the LORD, and Satan standing at his right hand to accuse him. And the LORD said to Satan, "The LORD rebuke you, O Satan! The LORD who has chosen Jerusalem rebuke you! Is not this a brand plucked from the fire?"* (Zechariah 3:1-2).

What follows recounts how God in His mercy comes to us, to do for us what we cannot do for ourselves. In the very presence of failure, brokenness, and helplessness, the Angel of the LORD, standing next to Joshua, commands that He be made right and holy, purified by a sovereign act, based on the righteousness and mercy of God Himself.

> *Now Joshua was standing before the angel, clothed with filthy garments. And the angel said to those who were standing before him, "Remove the filthy garments from him." And to him he said, "Behold, I have taken your iniquity away from you, and I will clothe you with pure vestments." And I said, "Let them put a clean turban on his head." So they put a clean turban on his head and clothed him with garments. And the angel of the LORD was standing by* (Zechariah 3:3-5).

We are God's people, connected to Him in ways we have not yet comprehended. This truth has been revealed to us through Scripture, but we are only recently gaining fuller understanding of this incredible mystery that was hidden from the prophets, a glorious unfolding of God's purposes that even the angels do not completely understand.

Paul tells us, in First Corinthians 6:17, that a person *"joined to the Lord is one spirit with Him."* This does not refer to unity that is hopeful thinking or romantic idealism; it is an organic connection; a relationship of personalities; a oneness based in love and acceptance and intimate communion. Through the new birth offered by our gracious God, we become actual, bona-fide members of God's family, the original reality He had in mind from eternity past. He has always desired family; He has always had in His great heart this union of love between Himself and His created people.

We have become a holy people with a new nature. We are born of God, created, as it were, by His seed—the Lord Jesus Christ. Because we are "in Christ," we have become and will become like Him. We are able to carry His presence within us. We have been given so many precious promises that we now are exhorted to remember what He has done for us and given to us: *"...perfecting holiness in the fear of the Lord"* (2 Corinthians 7:1). We have been made a temple of the Holy Spirit who is in us; we have been purchased by the priceless blood of Jesus; we carry the seed of promise and glory within us, because, like young Mary, who responded to the word and the will of God, we too respond to the Lover of our souls with the proclamation: *"Let it be to me according to your word."*

ORIGINS OF THIS BOOK

In the summer and fall of 2017, the Holy Spirit began speaking prophetically to His people in many nations concerning a forty-day period of consecration. As weeks passed, more and more believers connected with each other and discovered that countless people were experiencing the same stirring. A number of us began to pray more intentionally to discover what specifically God was saying to us. He revealed that He desired a time which He would perform a work of preparation and consecration in the lives of His faithful remnant. As we collectively shared with each other and sought the Lord regarding this time, we longed for language that would best describe what we were sensing deep within His heart. It seemed to be something more intense and powerful than would be expressed by the word consecration, which means to be set apart; although that is vital and precious, we realized that God intended to take us further to a place of being united in oneness of spirit with Him. We began to hear the word "yielding," and we realized that the forty days were to be a time of yielding to the Lord in order to become one with Him in a way we had never yet experienced.

The Spirit spoke to us that this time of yielding was to begin November 11 and continue through December 20, which that year coincided with the final day of Hanukkah. He then led us to three portions of Scripture to reveal His intention for the forty days.

The first portion we focused on was Zechariah 3 that gives the account of the changing of Joshua the high priest's garments, and the removal of the accusations that had soiled them. We knew that the Spirit would do the same for us as individuals and as families. So many of us had "worn" accusations because we believed them, and therefore had come into agreement with lies and considered them to be truth; but in reality the accusations were not against us, but against our Father. Those lies had soiled our garments and wounded our unity with the One who chose us. God invited us to stand before Him in quietness and solitude, to allow Him to remove accusations that were like soiled garments. We realized He would remove accusations against the truth of His character and His faithfulness, and we would be restored to "one spirit with Christ" (1 Corinthians 6:17).

The second portion of Scripture was found in Luke 1:38, when the angel of the Lord appeared to Mary, announcing that she would conceive a child as the Holy Spirit came upon her. She responded, *"Behold the maidservant of the Lord! Let it be to me according to your word"* (Luke 1:38).

This became the focal point of our posture of yielding to what He had spoken. We believed the Spirit of God would come upon us during the forty days, to clothe us with new garments and to restore our authority, which was weakened as we allowed accusations against His holiness and truth to soil our lives and our families.

The third portion of Scripture God led us to focus on reminded us of His sovereign authority and power to perform His purposes. It was found in Zechariah 4:6: *So he answered and said to me: "This is the word of the Lord to Zerubbabel: 'Not by might nor by power, but by My Spirit,' says the Lord of hosts."*

It was vital for us to understand that we were not entering into a work of the flesh but a gift of mercy from the Lord. We were to yield, but the Holy Spirit would sovereignly accomplish all that was in His heart. Our yielding was not to consist of anguished self-examination, but instead be a daily surrender of humble trust, inviting and allowing the Holy Spirit to come upon us in order to accomplish the will of God in our lives.

To help encourage the body throughout the forty days, we sensed the Holy Spirit prompting us to write daily devotionals that were posted on the "Watchmen for the Nations" website, where they were translated into various languages. This was one of many ways the global community of believers was able to remain connected in purpose and vision throughout the time of consecration.

A number of people commented to us "You should put these devotions in a book!" After prayer and counsel with trusted friends and associates, we determined that "it seemed good to the Holy Spirit and to us" that we should revise and expand the original daily thoughts into the book you are now reading.

TAKING PART IN *THE YIELDING*

When we read the accounts in Scripture of God's activity in the lives of people, we become aware how powerfully He works through submitted, humble vessels. Joshua's restoration and purification were a result of the Lord's sovereign act. Joshua did nothing but stand, helpless and guilty, while the Lord performed what needed to be done. Mary yielded as God's maidservant, to allow His holy will to be accomplished. They both experienced the sovereign touch of God, even though they had done nothing to deserve it.

As a group of believers taking part in the forty days, we found that it was a healing time for many in the body of Christ as we yielded in a new and fresh way to His authority. There were testimonies of the Lord accomplishing amazing things among us, things we were not able to do for ourselves.

In keeping with the rhythm of the original offerings, this book is broken up into five segments of eight chapters. Each segment considers the themes that God revealed to us during that time. They are an inspirational invitation to assist you as you read and yield your heart. The book can be read through as an organic unity, with the various chapters building upon one another to a conclusion. It can also be used as a devotional by reading a set number of chapters per day, entering into the experience in much the same way that we did during that time. You may wish to use the topics as points for discussion or prayer in small groups.

We encourage you to consider partaking in communion as often as the Spirit leads you as you make your way through the book. It can be an integral part of aligning with truth and yielding to the presence of the Lord.

As you read and ponder the insights God reveals to you, you will find that yielding in a fresh and greater way than ever before will allow Him to not only restore understanding of your true identity, but it will also restore and deepen the revelation in your heart of *His* true identity. Recognizing who He is, and who you truly are to Him, will enable your mind to be renewed, your hope refreshed, your intimacy restored, your passion reignited, and your God-given authority reestablished!

Right now, determine to make this a "set apart" time, and ask the Holy Spirit to lead you and teach you, comforting and convicting you with His presence and wisdom that gives you hope and desire and strength to be renewed. Ask Him to begin to reveal and remove all accusations that have been raised against the knowledge of the Holy One in your life. It is vital to have this perspective: *The root of all accusations you have believed and agreed with are first and foremost accusations against the character and faithfulness of God.* This is not something to feel ashamed of or condemned about; the Lord does not desire to chastise you for your lack; instead, He will **now** remove these iniquities that have soiled His sons' and daughters' lives and robbed them of the authority that He created them to rule and reign in.

Yielding is a powerful posture that brings you into the safety and intimate care of the One who has all authority and holds all power in the Universe. Yielding will prove to be a springboard into a renewed mind and a greater trust in the mercy of your heavenly Father of Lights, who sets you free and catapults you into oneness with Jesus that is beyond what you could ever have dreamed possible.

> ***Now to Him who is able to do exceedingly abundantly above all that we ask or think, according to the power that works in us, to Him be glory in the church by Christ Jesus to all generations, forever and ever. Amen.***
> (Ephesians 3:20-21).

Prologue: A Vision in the Night

Jerusalem, 519 B.C.

The people had returned from Babylon, land of punishment and sorrow, land of discipline and mourning. We had languished and despaired; we wailed and poured out our hearts and lifted our hands to ADONAI*; but how could we sing His songs in a foreign land? How could we lift our eyes in hope, we who had disobeyed and spurned the love of Israel's husband? Our sin turned the heavens to brass.*

But as the prophets foretold, ADONAI *returned us to the Land of Promise. We returned as dreamers; we returned as those once again freed from slavery and bondage, just as we had been freed generations earlier from Egypt. We returned rejoicing, celebrants at a wedding feast, our mouths drenched with the water and wine of laughter and song—we who had eaten the dust of adultery, our hopeless, shriveled tongues tasting bitter rejection.*

So, we returned, and began construction on the Temple to house our God. But we who had been delivered by so great a miracle, by the strong hand of ADONAI, *found numerous and diverse obstacles and opposition and our hands grew faint with discouragement; it became enough for us to attend to our own troubles and work to provide our own houses and livelihoods, and so work on the Temple stalled as the hearts of the people grew weak and their zeal and passion grew cold. The House of* ADONAI *lay in ruins, and His people excused themselves, saying to one another "the time has not yet come to rebuild."*

And I, Zechariah ("ADONAI remembers"), *born in Babylon, born in servitude, released into freedom in the land of our fathers, prophesied to the people, along with the elder prophet Haggai, encouraging them to remain faithful in submission to the hope and the commandments of our God, who is forever faithful and exalted above the heaven of heavens. By the word of* ADONAI, *we commanded the people to return to God and not to follow the unrighteous ways of our forefathers, who had sinned and caused our captivity in the foreign land. We encouraged the people to complete the task of building the Temple.*

In the night visions, ADONAI *showed me many wonders and commanded me to speak to the people. I was given visions to speak rebuke, but also to give comfort and encouragement. In one of these, I saw Joshua, the* kohen gadol, *who represented our people before the majesty of our eternal Lord. But he was not clothed in garments prescribed by* ADONAI*; he was dressed in clothes filthy with dung and spattered with uncleanness and vile failure. He stood trembling as the adversary, the satan, stood and catalogued his sins and the sins of the people, and blasphemed* ADONAI *who lives forever.*

But beside Joshua, the Angel –ADONAI *stood, in His brilliant and radiating purity, and spoke over the head of the priest to the foul and bitter creature bringing charge.*

"ADONAI *rebukes you, satan. Indeed* ADONAI, *who has chosen Jerusalem, rebukes you. Is not this man a brand plucked out of the fire?"*

Then I saw Him command angels to clothe Joshua in new finery, the pure linen priestly garments, and place the turban on his head that proclaimed him set apart unto ADONAI.

O ADONAI, *we Your people were covered in shame and weakness, disobedience and failure; but our God is greater than all our iniquity, and You raise up our limp hands and make strong our feeble knees. We do not trust in our strength, but in Your mighty power, for you are above the highest heavens. Although You are very great and beyond the understanding of any of the sons of men, yet You continue to proclaim to us that You are with us, and that You will bless us. You are our God, who declares to us that "though our sins be like scarlet, You will make us as white as snow."*

<u>SECTION ONE</u>

Freed From Accusation and the Land of Bondage

<u>Zechariah 3:1-2</u>

Then the angel showed me Joshua the high priest standing before the angel of the LORD. The accuser, satan, was there at the angel's right hand, making accusations against Joshua. And the LORD said to satan, "I, the LORD, reject your accusations, satan. Yes, the LORD, who has chosen Jerusalem, rebukes you. This man is like a burning stick that has been snatched from the fire."

The LORD Himself rejects satan's accusations against us and rebukes him for his lies and assault against us, the people God has redeemed.

Our Father reminds us that our lives have been purchased by grace, and that by grace His call upon our lives will be accomplished. We find courage and identity in the true knowledge of God.

1

Beginnings

Then he showed me Joshua the kohen gadol *standing before the angel of* ADONAI *and the satan, standing at his right hand to accuse him.* ADONAI *said to the satan, "*ADONAI *rebukes you, the satan. Indeed* ADONAI, *who has chosen Jerusalem, rebukes you. Is not this man a brand plucked out of the fire?"* (Zechariah 3:1-2, TLV)

You have been born into a world engaged in cosmic war. From the beginning of mankind's history there has existed an enemy, a wicked being that is determined to rage against God and all that is good and right and flourishing. In the passage above, the original Hebrew refers to this foul creature as *"the satan,"* which means "an adversary, the one who resists." This is the serpent that deceived Eve with its seductive promises, which in actuality were lies and accusations against the goodness and faithfulness of God. Hell and the demonic realm will use any opportunity to attempt to slander the Almighty and accuse His creation.

The enemy is relentless and tireless in his accusations against us, desiring to ruin our hope and our trust in the love of Jesus. He wants to weaken us, so that we are not able to stand in the evil day, and having done all, to stand (Galatians 6). But our Lord's passionate intention is to address this accuser who brings indictments against us, the beloved ones whom Jesus died for. God also deals with accusations against His character, because the more the adversary can deceive people into believing that the Creator is, in fact, not good and not to be trusted, the more he can ruin God's beautiful creation and short-circuit human flourishing, which brings abundance and proper order to the earth.

As we begin this journey of "yielding," it is important that we take time to allow the Holy Spirit to search our hearts and reveal accusations we have believed that have come against us and against our heavenly Father. These lies that we have believed become like the filthy garments worn by Joshua the high priest in Zechariah's vision. When we agree with satan's defilement and whisperings, lies and hopelessness take root within us, infecting our minds and enervating our souls.

Because our enemy is relentless, many of us have labored for years under false beliefs that are regularly strengthened through our misapprehension of circumstances and spiritual warfare. But we have an Advocate, greater in determination than the enemy, unimaginably powerful and wiser than eternity, who has promised to lead us into all truth. The Holy Spirit is our guide and as we set ourselves on the path to wisdom and yielding, He will help us break every agreement with lies and darkness. He will rebuke the enemy and silence the accusations. He will remove the tattered rags we have worn for so long and replacing them with clean, white garments.

We are at a point in history that we recognize the time of the culmination of God's purposes is growing very near. The hour is late; the Bridegroom is coming soon; and as people longing for the return of the Lord Jesus, we want to be as the five wise virgins (Matthew 25). This is a critical time in history; it is not a time to be careless or foolish, or be caught sleeping. The body of Christ is needed as never before to speak life and hope to the confusion that exists in the nations of the world. As we noted in the introduction, God will do for us what we cannot do for ourselves. This has always been His good intention; but the gravity of the hour should cause us to understand the great honor and privilege God has given us to be alive in this hour, people who are on the earth "for such a time as this."

The journey to greater yielding is a path into oneness with Jesus that is beyond anything you could have dreamed possible. The Lord will demonstrate in your life His work, accomplished by His Spirit, and you will understand His pronouncement in Zechariah 4:6, *"Not by might nor by power, but by My Spirit," says the Lord of hosts.*

2

The Gift of Vulnerability

For many years, I (Jeffrey) loved the words of Jesus in John 15. I was comforted by the idea of Him being the Vine from whom my life sprang. I was one of many branches, and while I didn't relish any "pruning" processes, I always understood that it was for my good. I heartily agreed with verse five: *"I am the vine, you are the branches. He who abides in Me, and I in him, bears much fruit; for without Me you can do nothing."*

This is such a wonderful truth. But through my mental grid, every time I read and pondered that statement, I would think, "Yes, it is so true, Lord. Without you, there is very little I am able to do."

It took many years and countless failures for me to begin to grasp the fact that when Jesus said "...without Me you can do nothing," what He actually meant was that I could do **nothing**. In the original Greek, the word is *oudeis*, which is "*...a powerful negating conjunction. It...leaves no exceptions.*"[1]

We do not like to admit this. We feel we should be strong and capable; we think it is a badge of honor to be able to accomplish good things in our spheres of influence. And of course, we were created to oversee and tend to creation. There is genuine satisfaction in our ability to flourish and grow in our gifts and talents. But humble satisfaction and

---

[1] Bible Hub; "oudeis and outheis, oudemia, ouden and outhen," *Strong's Concordance*, accessed February 27, 2018, https://biblehub.com/greek/3762.htm.

gratitude to our Creator for His good gifts in us has been perverted into innate hunger for power and control. We like accomplishments because they make us feel strong. Even our growth in godly living can subtly entice us into complacency and conceit. Then Jesus, in His matchless way, comes along and obliterates our self-satisfaction in a single phrase. *"You can do nothing."* He is kind and gracious, too faithful in His love for us to let us continue in the self-deception that leads us to think we are accomplishing any spiritual growth through our efforts.

The naked truth is that we are dependent upon Him for everything: every tiny act of obedience, every move towards faithfulness, every faltering prayer of faith.

> ***We must learn of Jesus...it is the indwelling Christ who will live in us this life...The root of all virtue and grace, of all faith and acceptable worship, is that we know that we have nothing but what we receive, and bow in deepest humility to wait upon God for it.***
>
> —Andrew Murray, ***Humility & Absolute Surrender***

With this understanding, we allow the Lord to bring us into this time dedicated to Him, allowing us to be set apart. It begins with the Holy Spirit speaking these words over us: *"I am about to do for you what you have not been able to do for yourself."* He invites us to understand our inability and our vulnerability. Sometimes we feel as though it is our choice whether or not to be vulnerable; with other people, that may be true, but before the One who is all-seeing, our souls are stripped naked and we are vulnerable, even if we choose not to perceive our true condition.

This recognition may cause you to feel uncomfortable at first, because your old self-woven garments of protection and guardedness must be removed; but the Lord's invitation is a wooing into deeper intimacy. He will enable you to encounter the deep, hidden recesses of pain and fear that have held you back from Him and from greater unity with His people. Vulnerability becomes the most beautiful gift you have ever received as you experience a new depth of oneness with your Creator. He exposes us in order to cover and heal those places that have not yet been fully His, so that He can make room for more of His presence. You will be taken into His heart and into the mysteries of His beauty in ways you never dreamed possible.

> *And to us who have fled for refuge to lay hold upon the hope that is set before us in the gospel, how unutterably sweet is the knowledge that our heavenly Father knows us completely. No talebearer can inform on us, no enemy can make an accusation stick....He knew us utterly before we knew Him and called us to Himself in the full knowledge of everything that was against us...His knowledge of our afflictions and adversities is more than theoretic; it is personal, warm and compassionate. Whatever may befall us, God knows and cares as no one else can.*
> —A.W. Tozer, *The Knowledge of the Holy*

Draw life from Him, for He is fully trustworthy and completely capable. His love and mercy are infinite. His passion for you is unwavering and relentless. He will never take advantage of our weakness, for He delights in showing us His kindness and manifest power.

3

Let Go and Let God

Ever since Adam and Eve succumbed to the temptation to try to be "like God, knowing good and evil," the rest of us now live with a natural bent to demand that we be in control. Our daily situations seem to teach us that letting go of control is to be "out of control." For many people, that is the ultimate horror; it seems we would do almost anything to maintain control of our lives, our surroundings, our destinies. Yet, letting go in order to let God be in control is the very yielding that allows transformation to begin.

As His sons and daughters we understand that the Father's ways and His wisdom are higher than the ways and wisdom of man. As you surrender to the work of the Holy Spirit, you will find that you are enabled to let go of all that holds you back from the full experience of being one spirit with Him. Surrender escorts you into yielding that says, "Not my will but your will be done."

God is looking for a people who trust Him more than they fear not having control. They have learned—have tasted and seen that the LORD is good—that God is faithful and righteous in all His ways. Those who have surrendered all control over to Him have learned that His statues and truths have become the pathway into freedom and rest, because they have witnessed that the ways of God are proven and sure. Giving God full control in both the mountains and valleys will assure that you are carried by the arms of peace to the victory that awaits you.

The only thing required of you is surrender. Our King Jesus is a victorious warrior, and He won for us a magnificent, eternal victory. But the path to that victory first involved waving a white flag of surrender. Jesus knelt in Gethsemane, the majestic Eternal God submitting Himself to the will of the Father. Our fallen world's systems advance through power and manipulation, but the kingdom of God shatters the gates of hell through love and humility and sacrificial obedience. Jesus showed us the example of having no thought for His own welfare, no consideration of grasping after His own deserved glory.

He has given us the Holy Spirit to teach us and empower us to follow with the same heart. In 1896, Judson W. Van DeVenter and Winfield S. Weeden beautifully expressed this when they published the now-classic hymn "I Surrender All":

All to Jesus I surrender,
Make me, Savior, wholly Thine;
Let me feel Thy Holy Spirit,
Truly know that Thou art mine.
I surrender all; I surrender all.
All to Thee, my blessed Savior,
I surrender all.

By the power of the Holy Spirit, you are able to surrender all; hold nothing back. He is worthy of all of you—your strengths and your weaknesses. He is the One who calms the storms in the winter seasons and gives you a drink of cool water in the heat of the summer. He is your maker and it is only in the place of full surrender to the Potter's hand that we become what He originally fashioned us to be. "Make me, Savior, wholly Thine!"

But now, O Lord, You are our Father,
We are the clay, and You our potter;
And all of us are the work of Your hand
(Isaiah 64:8).

Within His hands everything thrives and is blessed. When we grasp for and try to cling to what we feel should belong to us, we limit ourselves to what we can understand, and our lives are ultimately stunted and empty. We become like a painting barely begun; a canvas with little daubs and splotches of paint. But when we surrender to the Master, everything we give to Him is crafted into beauty and our lives become transformed into a masterpiece.

4

You are the Apple of God's Eye

"Just as a father protects his children or a man protects the bride of his youth, so I watch over My children and My bride with a fierce and jealous love. You are the apple of My eye!"

The cries of sons and daughters who have faced fierce and lonely battles are heard by our heavenly Father. Your desperate pleas for restoration and relief do not vanish into uncaring emptiness. God is always present and listening with complete attention, and He will respond despite our desperate circumstances and reach past our dark emotions. He is powerful to draw us up from the miry pit of despair and failure and free us into joy and trust.

David knew this situation, and he knew that his gracious Lord would rescue him.

I waited patiently and expectantly for the Lord,
and He inclined to me and heard my cry.
He drew me up out of a horrible pit—a pit of tumult
and of destruction—
out of the miry clay (froth and slime) and set
my feet upon a rock,
steadying my steps and establishing my goings.
And He has put a new song in my mouth, a song of praise

to our God.
Many shall see and fear—revere, and worship—and put their trust and confident reliance in the Lord
(Psalm 40:1-3, AMP).

When the devil tries to assault or frighten us or steal our promises and peace, the Father releases His voice in response: with tender compassion to the hearts of His children; with a terrifying roar against satan, like thunder above the clash and chaos of the battle, routing the enemy as the Almighty arises to protect and guard those He loves out of the depths of His infinite heart. One of the names of our glorious God is **YHVH-Shamar** –the Lord our Keeper (Psalm 121)!

> *No part of the body more precious, more tender, and more carefully guarded than the eye; and of the eye, no portion more peculiarly to be protected than the central apple, the pupil, or as the Hebrew calls it, 'the daughter of the eye.' The all-wise Creator has placed the eye in a well-protected position; it stands surrounded by projecting bones like Jerusalem encircled by mountains.*
> —Charles Spurgeon, *The Treasury of David, Volume I*

God proclaims you His dearly cherished one; He has come to restore you, to refresh you, and to keep you and your loved ones.

Keep me as the apple of your eye;
hide me in the shadow of your wings,
from the wicked who do me violence,
my deadly enemies who surround me
(Psalm 17:-9).

Though the enemy has surrounded many of God's sons and daughters with threats and adversity, attempting to intimidate them and frighten them with a display of force and ferocity, it is

God Himself who sets a table for His children in the presence of their enemies. Though the thief has stolen, it is the Lord who will restore double. Although the accuser has taunted with his many mockeries, it is God who will rebuke him.

> *You prepare a table before me*
> *in the presence of my enemies;*
> *you anoint my head with oil;*
> *my cup overflows.*
> *Surely goodness and mercy shall follow me*
> *all the days of my life,*
> *and I shall dwell in the house of the LORD forever*
> (Psalm 23:5-6).

Whoever touches you touches the *apple of His eye*. God will not be mocked and He will not allow His beloved to be touched or wounded without vindicating her and punishing the enemy. He is watching over the great transformational work that is occurring in you the same way He orchestrated and carefully attended to the work done in the life of Joshua the high priest (Zechariah 3).

One late spring morning I (Jeffrey) was praying when suddenly, the presence of the Holy Spirit overwhelmed me and I felt His word erupt from me; it truly seemed like a roar released from the heart of the Lion of Judah. It was a strong encouragement to me personally, but I knew it was also His pronouncement for all His people, to strengthen us for the coming days:

"I am moving you forward for the sake of My Kingdom. You are ***mine!*** *Hear Me roaring over you: 'MINE!' I am fiercely protective of the work I have done and am continuing to do. I am watching over your life with exquisite care. Do you not know? Have you not heard? I will never fail or forsake you!"*

He is consuming fire who burns with unquenchable passion for us, and He will not be dissuaded or discouraged in His relentless zeal to bring us into all the fullness of Christ Jesus. Nothing that occurs in your life escapes His attention; He who knows when every sparrow falls to the ground never removes His loving, protective gaze from you.

> *We may take comfort from hence, that our sincerity cannot be unknown to an infinite under-standing. Not a way of the righteous is concealed from him...God knows the least dram of grace and righteousness in the hearts of his people, though but as a smoking flax, or the least bruise of a saving conviction, and knows it so as to cherish it; he knows that work he hath begun, and never hath his eye off from it to abandon it.*
> —Stephen Charnock, *The Existence and Attributes of God*

Every enemy that rises against you will be punished. *For thus said the Lord of hosts, after his glory sent me to the nations who plundered you, for he who touches you touches the apple of his eye....* (Zechariah 2:8).

This verse speaks specifically about Jerusalem, but there is application to His chosen people as well, both Jew and Gentile. Vindication belongs to the Lord, so as we hide in the shelter of His wing, we rest assured that our great Guardian is with us, hiding our lives in His mighty hands. Our King rules over us with justice, gentleness, and mercy.

> *The Father has given judgment to the Lamb that was slain, in order to be fully available to us as the 'Father of compassion,' the God of all comfort. Do you actually believe that anything in this world could ever snatch you out of His hand? The Father surely will not let go of you, unless you choose to run away from Him; He is an abyss of compassion!*
> —Geri Keller, *Father—A Look into the Heart of God*

When the Father Held My Hair Back

When I was a young woman I dealt with the eating disorder bulimia. After fifteen years of failed attempts, on my own and with help from friends and family, to overcome this "pain and shame driven" disorder, I found myself in a sixty-day treatment center to save my life. Upon my release I felt empowered to live in recovery but this "recovery" was short lived. When pain came knocking at the door of my life again I quickly returned to my old companion that would bring me temporary relief by bringing a false sense of control.

As a child, I was exposed to emotional and physical abuse. Our family situation was chaotic and the emotional pain and physical fear would often cause me to hide in the bathroom where the locked door seemed to be a safe hiding place. When my dad was in a rage I would run to the bathroom and if I was able to make it there and lock the door before he could reach me to punish me, then I was safe. I'd stay behind the locked door until he'd have enough to drink to calm him down. Over the years this "hiding place" became the place where an eating disorder evolved. Throwing up my pain caused me to feel a euphoric sense of control over my raging fear and out-of-control emotions; though I couldn't control the chaos around me I felt as though I could take temporary control over the chaos within. Momentary relief became a pattern of life that carried me into a dangerous place where it controlled me.

After the lengthy and expensive stay in the treatment center ended in yet another failure, I was thrown into depression that left me in despair and finally drove me to a suicide attempt. The people around me were overwhelmed with concern and I was overwhelmed with facing another moment of pain.

One day, during this dark time, while I was home alone, the pain came upon me with its familiar rage and torment. I ran to the bathroom (my hiding place) in order to feel safe and to gain control. As I closed and locked the door I heard an almost audible voice speak to me saying, "Daughter, leave the door open and let me in."

I knew that this was the voice of my heavenly Father and struggled to even consider letting Him into this place that had been the only safe place I had known. I stood there and heard the voice again, "Open the door and let Me in."

His voice was so tender that I finally responded. I opened the door but still proceeded with kneeling in front of the toilet to rid myself of the pain. If God was in there with me, what would He think of what I was about to do. Would He be angry and abandon me? Would He leave and never come back? As I bent over the toilet I suddenly felt hands reach from behind me to hold my hair back. I knew that these were not human hands but the hands of a father who loved me just as I was. As these hands held my hair back the voice of God spoke ever so tenderly, ***"From now on I will always be here with you."***

As soon as I heard those words I fell to the ground in tears. My Father held me there for a long time, allowing all of the fear and pain to pour out. I had let my Father in and it was safe. In the midst of my pain, He came in, completely unashamed of me. His only desire was to hold me and let me know that I am not alone. In that moment I was delivered from the eating disorder. I had opened my heart when I yielded to His request to let Him come in. When I opened the bathroom door I also opened my heart's door.

He is a safe Father and a good Father who receives you right where you are. He meets you in your pain and takes away the shame. Is He asking you to open the door and let Him in? If so, yield to His desire and what you experience will set you free.

~Kathi Pelton

5

The LORD Fights for You

Our King who shed His blood is a victorious Warrior. In the magnificent Messianic Psalm 45, the writer calls out,

> *Gird Your sword upon Your thigh, O Mighty One,*
> *With Your glory and Your majesty...*
> *Your arrows are sharp in the heart of the*
> *King's enemies....* (Psalm 45:3, 5).

Jesus, the Lamb who was slain, is now exalted as our risen King who has all authority and all power, having vanquished every enemy that stands against the kingdom of God. Nothing can oppose Him! He won the victory for us; He has risen from the dead as "firstfruits" for all who will follow, and now He commissions us to go in His authority and continue to advance His reign. For, as Paul reveals:

> *For since by man came death, by Man also came the resurrection of the dead. For as in Adam all die, even so in Christ all shall be made alive. But each one in his own order: Christ the firstfruits, afterward those who are Christ's at His coming. Then comes the end, when*

He delivers the kingdom to God the Father, when He puts an end to all rule and all authority and power.
For He must reign till He has put all enemies under His feet (1 Corinthians 15:21-25).

We are aware that up to this present hour, we are engaged in epic warfare for the lives of people for whom Jesus died. We can see a picture of this great battle over our lives and destinies in Zechariah 3:1.

Then he showed me Joshua the high priest standing before the Angel of the LORD, and satan standing at his right hand to oppose him.

Satan stood on the opposite side of Joshua from where the Lord stood "in order to oppose him" (the Hebrew word is a primitive root from which "satan" is derived, and it means to accuse, persecute and oppose. The definition of *oppose* is "...to place as an obstacle; to put in opposition, with a view to counterbalance or countervail, and thus to hinder, defeat, destroy, or prevent effect. To act against; to resist, by physical force, by arguments, or by other means...."[2]

Satan actively resists and opposes God's purposes for your life. The enemy attempts to persuade you to agree with his lies, so that you, too, resist the plans of God and give assent to his arguments against God's faithfulness, His character, the truth of His Word, and the kind intentions of His will. Satan, the father of lies, is a foul rebel that hates God and refuses to comply with His ways, so he continually shouts arguments of opposition against truth.

[2] *Webster's New Twentieth-Century Dictionary* (Unabridged), s.v. "oppose."

Yielding requires humility, humbling yourself before your humble King who never opposes you but graciously receives you just as you are. In contrast, the enemy, in great pride, continually seeks to shift the church away from alignment with God's character through opposition and accusation.

The moment that a believer comes into agreement with an accusation that opposes God's truth, he or she has become aligned with a lie. All these lies of accusation—whether they are about yourself, another person, an entire group, or even a situation—are ultimately rooted in a accusations against the Lord Himself. They are echoes of the mocking serpent's voice that spoke to Adam and Eve, questioning the fidelity and goodness of God. When you believe a lie, you become aligned with the accuser in that lie.

In all of our years of writing publicly, we have received hundreds, if not thousands, of letters from disillusioned Christians who have aligned their beliefs with lies from the enemy. They will tell us about how God has not treated them justly; they will tell us the negative lies that they believe about themselves, their spouses, their children, or their churches. It always grieves us and we cannot imagine the pain that it brings to the heart of God who loves every individual with immeasurable love. God is very intentional about breaking the lies that stem from accusation and opposition off His people because the lies become open doors in lives for the enemy to gain access. He will quickly come in and occupy places within their hearts while making plans to take further ground.

While Kathi was meditating on the first verses in Zechariah 3, she was taken into a vision, and saw Joshua standing between the Lord and satan. In this vision, Joshua was no longer content to stand in the middle of two opinions. Instead, he rushed to the Lord and as he did he came into absolute alignment with Him. As he embraced Jesus he no longer heard the accusations and words of opposition that the enemy had continually shouted at him. She saw Joshua embrace the beauty of oneness with Christ, which became like a shield around him.

Yield to truth! Allow yourself to run into the arms of Truth. You can determine that you will no longer allow yourself to halt and stagger helplessly, confused as you consider different options. Ponder the words of Elijah the prophet, who stood on Mount Carmel and fearlessly said to the people of Israel, who had gathered to witness the showdown between baal and *ADONAI*, *"How long will you go limping between two different opinions? If the LORD is God then follow him..."* (1 Kings 18:21).

To follow Christ is to follow truth. Yield to the truth that will set you free from every accusation and clothe you anew in clean garments.

6

Not By Might...

"You're making a mountain out of a molehill."

Almost all of us have said (or at least thought) this expression when faced with someone's overreaction at what seems to be a trivial event. Most likely, we have also been guilty of this distorted viewpoint from time to time when faced with what appear to be insurmountable challenges. Satan and the forces of darkness are quick to capitalize on our insecurities, failures, and fears by whispered suggestions and exaggerations about our circumstances and our lack of resource to deal with the trials that come into our lives.

But keep in mind, God has never told us that the battle is to be won through our own strength or cleverness. Young David shouted this truth to the enemies of Israel when he faced Goliath: "*...the Lord saves not with sword and spear. For the battle is the Lord's....*" (1 Samuel 17:47). God is greater than our enemies.

> *The Messenger-Angel said, "Can't you tell?" "No, sir," I said. Then he said, "This is God's Message to Zerubbabel: 'You can't force these things. They only come about through my Spirit,' says God-of-the-Angel-Armies. 'So, big mountain, who do you think you are? Next to Zerubbabel you're nothing but a molehill. He'll proceed to set the Cornerstone in place, accompanied by cheers: Yes! Yes! Do it!'"* (Zechariah 4:6, MSG).

"You can't force these things...So, big mountain...you're nothing but a molehill." In contrast to the fear-mongering of satan and our human obsession to control our lives due to fear, God turns our common expression on its head. (He is fond of doing such things.)

As you yield to the power and might of the Holy Spirit, you are enabled to look at the circumstances of your life—even those that appear to tower above you as mountains, menacing and powerful—as though they are molehills. Though the enemy wants to draw attention to shadows, the light of truth and the presence of the Father of Lights reveals that what we think are mountains are but molehills before Him. Your authority and identity as sons and daughters of the Most High God is terrifying to the enemy and every demonic force. They tremble in their ranks as the Cornerstone of Christ is securely placed in your life and you yield fully to His Spirit and to the will of your Father. The power of the Holy Spirit causes mountains to tremble and demons to flee. The voice of the Lord is powerful; His dominion is everlasting; His mercy is unending; His love is unreserved; His authority is absolute. Though the earth may be shaken, you will not be. You belong to Him; you have been rescued from the domain of darkness and carried by His love into His Kingdom that cannot be shaken (Colossians 1:13).

He has begun a good and powerful work in you. His foundation is strong and sure, for Jesus Himself is the cornerstone: the principal stone in the foundation of an edifice; the fundamental part of primary importance in a structure. Jesus has triumphed over sin and death. The Father is building us into a holy temple of His presence, and He has promised to give us all good things (Romans 8:32). With faith and authority, declare that Jesus is the Cornerstone of your life and the lives of your family members. Proclaim this truth to counter the lies of the enemy that would seek to place you back under bondage and condemnation. His accusations and the voices that attempt to seduce you to live in fear are lies; the all-sufficient corrective for satan's lies is the eternal truth of Scripture. Jesus, the King of kings is the Cornerstone of our lives.

> *...we have a great deal of comfort presented to us, in that Christ is presented for us as a stone, for there we shall find him, first,*

> *to be the foundation stone, nothing can stand which is not built upon Christ; secondly, to be a cornerstone, that unites things most disunited; and then to be the stone that Jacob slept upon; fourthly, to be the stone that David slew Goliath withal; and lastly to be such a stone as is a rock, and such a rock as no waters nor storms can remove or shake. These are benefits: Christ Jesus is a stone, no firmness but in him; a fundamental stone, no building but on him...no rest, no tranquility but in him...no defence against troubles and tribulations but in him.*
> —John Donne, *"Of Christ as Foundation and Cornerstone"*

Hear the Lord speaking over your life with awesome authority the words from Zechariah 3:2: And the Lord said to satan, "The Lord rebuke you, O satan! The Lord who has chosen Jerusalem rebuke you! Is not this a brand plucked from the fire?"

God will not be mocked and He will rebuke the one that has accused and harassed you, your family, and His people. His pronouncement cannot, and will not, be challenged or refuted. You belong to Him, chosen and dearly beloved.

Jesus is the Cornerstone of your life!

7

From Regret to Restoration

"If only...."

Two small words, freighted with sorrow, often laden with desperation or despair. How often have you spoken those words, tormented and weakened with regret? You agonize at your memories of past failures, broken promises, and faltering, fruitless efforts. Unwanted reminders and numbing regrets will often come just as you quiet your heart to pray. But they are not your thoughts; they are the whispering taunts of the accuser who does not want you to forget what lies behind, but instead focus on the wreckage of your past. He wants to steal your time in the secret place of intimacy with Jesus.

This upheaval causes many believers to stay busy with frantic activity, because stopping long enough to quiet their souls often opens the floodgates of regret and thoughts of "If only..."

If only I had...

- been a more patient parent
- been a more loving spouse
- been more generous
- been more loving
- been more faithful
- been a better friend....

And the list goes on (and on!) Yet if we stop long enough for our souls to finish reviewing a dreadful "laundry list" of regrets, then we will find at the end that the Spirit of the Lord speaks to us a new list—a list of His attributes and mercies; a list of restoration.

I AM...
- a perfect Father who is patient with you
- a passionate Bridegroom who sees only your beauty
- a generous Father who holds nothing back from you
- a loving God who gave His all for you
- an ever present helper in your times of need
- a faithful friend....

And *His* list is true, and *His* list goes on, and on...and on into eternity. For all that we lack He is more than enough. There are no regrets in Christ Jesus; He came to us in our helplessness and brought restoration. He is the One who makes all things new (2 Corinthians 5:17; Revelation 21:5; Isaiah 43:19).

When we respond to the call of the Lord, we receive the blessing of His life-giving, life-restoring presence. Even when we sin, His conviction brings us to repentance and we are brought into a holy exchange, where we reap good things that we did not sow. The grace of God comes and changes us, forgiving and forgetting every iniquity. Our "if only" is exchanged for His "I AM." Regrets are washed away by the flood of restoration.

After Peter had denied Jesus three times, Scripture tells us he "wept bitterly." He came to the end of himself and his soul was consumed with the corrosion of regret. He had cursed and denied his Lord, just hours after proclaiming his loyalty even unto death!

But as we know, this was not the end to Peter's story. As his regrets turned to repentance, we discover Jesus' restorative response. Upon seeing Peter for the first time after His resurrection, Jesus' first desire was to restore him back to the intimacy that they shared. He first filled Peter's nets with fish, then He cooked him breakfast, and finally, He asked Peter three times, **"DO YOU LOVE ME?"**

Peter's three answers, each time affirming, "Yes, Lord, I love you!" became the restoration of his previous failure, his three denials.

The Lord has been doing this for men and women caught in the repercussions of regrets ever since that time. Many, like Peter, have come to the end of themselves. Some have denied Him during the "dark night" of their souls. Yet, after a night of weeping and sorrow, joy comes in the morning. Our God releases favor to us and sets a banqueting table of mercy and intimacy before us, even in the presence of our enemies of regret. He draws us into His new day and asks us the question that restores: **"DO YOU LOVE ME?"**

And we answer "YES! Yes! Yes! You know we love You!"

Love takes us in, makes us new, and gives us a home in His family and His heart. We truly can make this journey, from regret into repentance, and from there—joyfully—to restoration and the wonder of renewed relationship.

8

You Will be Transformed

Accusation, compromise, defeat, despair; these enemies have no right to torment the lives of those who belong to Christ. We yield to the truth that Jesus spoke regarding all who would follow Him: *"Therefore if the Son makes you free, you shall be free indeed"* (John 8:36). *"The words that I speak to you are spirit, and they are life"* (John 6:63). *"You are already clean because of the word which I have spoken to you"* (John 15:3).

So, you belong to the Lord Jesus Christ, the sovereign King of the universe; and He speaks these words over you: *"Where satan has tried to conform you to the world, I am about to transform you by My Spirit."*

We have this admonition and promise in Romans 12:2:

> *Do not conform to the pattern of this world, but be transformed by the renewing of your mind. Then you will be able to test and approve what God's will is—his good, pleasing and perfect will.*

This is a choice we make; to refuse the pressures of the world's systems and the thought-patterns of the world's wisdom. We understand that *"...we are from God, and the whole world lies in the power of the evil one"* (1 John 5:19); but we have been made new creations through Jesus, so we are no longer "laid out" under the sway of the devil and wickedness, as John describes the state of the world. We have the right to proclaim our freedom from bondage; the right to say "no" by the power of the Holy Spirit, who lives within us. We yield to Him by not allowing our lives and thoughts to be molded by human wisdom, nor by what our eyes see and our ears hear. Instead, we choose transformation by yielding to truth, which sets us free to be formed by God's supernatural handiwork.

As this occurs, you will be able to walk in the wisdom of knowing His will and walking in His ways. The Spirit of the Lord desires to transform every part of your life and mind that has previously been conformed to the culture of this world. The "wisdom" of the world clouds discernment, perverts judgment, and prevents understanding. As the Lord renews your mind it will bring you into a new clarity and wisdom.

> *And now, dear brothers and sisters, one final thing.*
> *Fix your thoughts on what is true, and honorable,*
> *and right, and pure, and lovely, and admirable.*
> *Think about things that are excellent and worthy of praise*
> (Philippians 4:8, NLT).

Yielding to the renewal of your mind will transform your life and the lives of those around you. Paul gives powerful, practical advice to see your mind renewed: Fix your thoughts on what is true, honorable, right, pure, lovely, and admirable. Doing this will cleanse your mind from the defilement of wicked and materialistic thinking, and will draw you into God's perspective. Dwelling on the negativity and fear that is part of unredeemed human experience causes depression, anxiety, rage, and disillusionment; such meditations will quickly align your soul with lies. Ask the Holy Spirit to help you to daily change your mind's "diet." Determine that you will fast from negative thinking, focusing on offense and all that is wrong with society around you, and dwelling on the fear that pervades so many lives.

We conclude the first section of *The Yielding* with the powerful and effective declaration that we have been freed from guilt and stain and condemnation. You have been freed by the Lord Jesus, who is Truth, and who cannot and will not lie. The accusations of the enemy have been rebuked by God Himself.

The world and its systems writhe with confusion, and the clamor from those who do not know the Lord are screams of unrest. But our Father is in charge, and He continues to call out for us to listen to Him for genuine wisdom and insight. He desires that we would have ears to hear what He speaks, and eyes to see what He sees. We yield to Him, filled with gratitude for the freedom He has provided for us.

Breakthrough for Malaysia

Malaysia has recently experienced a tremendous long-awaited breakthrough. It was, no doubt, a result of an accumulation of many people crying out to the Lord – from within Malaysia and beyond – fasting, praying, seeking God, and walking in obedience to the His leading. Ultimately of course, it was the Lord's doing and He deserves all the glory! But along the way, there were definitely numerous key times when the body of Christ in Malaysia yielded to the Lord in a very deliberate, tangible way.

One such pivotal time was in October 2017 when the Lord called believers from across the nation to come together, over several consecutive days, in four strategic locations. People paid a high price to adjust their schedules, pour out their finances, and fly from one city to the next. During this time, the Lord exposed the mocking spirit and the spirit of slumber that was prevalent over Malaysia. He warned us that the coming year was critical - from October 2017 to October 2018. He warned us that we needed to really cry out to Him for an awakening and that we needed to see and hear things first and foremost with our spiritual eyes and ears, not our natural ones. So we cried out to Him, that He would forgive us of our slumber, and that He would cleanse our eyes and ears. It was, indeed, a wakeup call to the body of Christ. We declared that no more would our God be mocked in our nation! The Lord also said that it would be a year of open doors that no man could shut, so with a new level of faith rising up from within, we committed to pressing in for the coming year, holding on to God and not letting go!

At one particular meeting during this time, when we were meeting up a mountain in a room packed full of leaders (particularly our native leaders) we declared into the spirit realm with all our hearts – "God, there is NO ONE like you! There is no one like You! You are the only true God! YOU created the heavens and earth! You are the God of heaven and You are the God of earth! So we say to all the other gods, take your place under the God of heaven! You have no power over the body of Christ!"

Then, starting on November 11, 2017, countless believers from across Malaysia joined in with a significant global "Forty-day Yielding" time. We entered into this time of yielding individually as well corporately. Towards the very beginning of the forty days, pastors and leaders gathered again (supported by key leaders from a few other nations) to really seek the Lord for the sake of our nation and to lay down our lives to Him afresh. During this time, among other things, the Lord highlighted 1 Corinthians 6:17 "But he who is joined to the Lord is one spirit with Him."

The day this gathering began, the Lord allowed me to personally experience something in the natural that would later be used to really hit home in the spiritual what this verse really means. That morning, as I had reached into our freezer to quickly grab something, all four of my fingers touched the bottom of the inside of our freezer and instantly froze to it! They were stuck in such an intense way that I knew there was no possibility of me pulling them back up, without serious damage. The pain rapidly escalated as we made a variety of unsuccessful attempts to free my hand from the relentless grip of our freezer. After using numerous strategies and much crying out to God, we finally managed to free my hand, but not without severe frostbite on all four fingers. For the next several days, my fingers were extremely swollen, excruciatingly painful, and could not be bent at all. Some parts had gone completely numb, while certain other parts had hypersensitive nerves, causing me to writhe in unbearable pain.

Later that day at the gathering of leaders, our friend David Demain explained that the Greek word used in 1 Corinthians 6:17 for "joined" is "kollao". This word does not refer to a weak or casual joining, but rather to glue together or fasten firmly together, in such a way that the two actually become inseparable. And, if the two actually do manage to be torn apart, there will be severe damage. So I had experienced in the natural with my fingers, exactly what we were talking about in the spiritual. We realized that as we were going through the "Forty-day Yielding," the Lord was wanting to glue (kollao) us together with Himself, so that we cannot go anywhere without Him anymore. So that we cannot departmentalize Him in our lives. We all continued on through our days together and throughout the remainder of the Forty-day Yielding with this vivid picture in our minds and with our hearts crying out for a deeper level of this inseparable bond with the Spirit.

The body of Christ in Malaysia continued yielding to the Lord, and crying out for His Kingdom to come and His will to be done in our nation. At that time, Malaysia had the third-longest ruling party in the world after North Korea and Communist China. The corruption and manipulation that had been running rampant, and the history of this undefeated government, made any change seem completely impossible in the natural. But leading up to our elections, with a new level of faith, the churches fasted and prayed around the clock, and countless nations contended with us for the impossible to become possible in our upcoming elections. On May 9, 2018, the day of our elections, Malaysia experienced an unprecedented breakthrough. Now instead of the mocking spirit running rampant over our nation, when people think of Malaysia they think of how a nation can be born in a day! We continue to praise God for what He has done! But we also want to continue to live our lives yielded to Him, so that He can continue to move in our nation, bringing her into the fullness of her destiny.

~Marilyn Ongkili

SECTION TWO

He Does What We Cannot

Zechariah 3:3-4

Joshua's clothing was filthy as he stood there before the angel. So the angel said to the others standing there, "Take off his filthy clothes." And turning to Joshua he said, "See, I have taken away your sins, and now I am giving you these fine new clothes."

The Lord performs His mercies and miracles of grace in our lives, and does for us what we are unable to do for ourselves. He removes our garments dirtied by sin—identities of failure and areas of compromise that cause shame, regret, and guilt. He clothes us anew in the righteousness of Christ.

The angel Gabriel visited Mary, announcing to her that she would be with child. She did not comprehend how that could happen, but she yielded herself fully to the will of the Father expressed by heaven's messenger. Although she was a young virgin, she was able to carry in her womb the Messiah—the wisdom and promise of God from all eternity. We too can posture ourselves like Mary, saying *"Be it unto me according to Your word,"* and we receive wisdom, discover renewed trust in His promises, and realize we are being transformed in the way we see ourselves and others.

9

Star of Wonder

O Star of wonder, star of night; star with royal beauty bright.
Westward leading, still proceeding, guide us to thy Perfect Light.

One of our favorite times of the year is the Christmas holiday season, because to us it is a reminder of the power and beauty of light. It is a joy that in the darkest part of the year (at least, in the northern hemisphere) the celebrations of Christmas and Hanukkah occur, bringing with them the cheerful delight of sparkling decorations and the comforting glow of candlelight. When we reflect on the beauty of light in these celebrations, it takes us back to the bright star in the sky two thousand years ago that proclaimed the birth of Messiah. That light led shepherds and wise men to the eternal Light who would offer deliverance to all mankind from the darkness of sin and death.

Most of the inhabitants of Bethlehem slept soundly in their beds, unaware that—even more than was true of Passover—this night was "not like other nights," because the Savior of the earth was born and laid in a manger. Mary surrendered herself to the word given her by Gabriel. Mary yielded to the will of God, and she was honored to carry and give birth to the Messiah. Filled with joy, she was able to proclaim that all generations would call her blessed, for the Mighty One had done great things for her (Luke 1:46-49). Profound obedience in a humble act of yielding set in motion the unfolding of a promise determined in the deep counsels of the

Almighty. Eternity would step into transience; the Uncreated would be fashioned in a virgin womb and birthed in lowliness.

But what a wonder was this unpretentious birth that changed not only Israel, but the whole earth. The heavens opened and praise and glory erupted from angelic hosts; the entire universe convulsed with joy that its King had appeared to bring restoration and deliverance to all creation. The holy and majestic Son of God descended from His throne of consuming fire to a shabby stable; the all-powerful King of Glory became helpless, tiny flesh, wet and red and squirming. The All-Sufficient left His throne and become fully dependent on those He Himself had created. The Mighty One became weak and vulnerable so that He might defeat darkness.

As we journey on this path of yielding, following the Light where He leads, just as the wise men knelt before the infant King, we prostrate ourselves in worship. We declare that this one is the true King and we are fully dependent upon Him. And as we glorify Him with our lives, we declare that all men and women should bow before Him and present their lives to Him.

Cry out to the Lord for more room in your heart. Call to the inhabitants in your city to be aware and cease from their spiritual slumber, for *"worship is what happens when people wake up"* (John Ortberg). The people and the angels of God still proclaim *"Glory to God in the highest!"* as we worship the King of kings and Lord of lords. He is life and His life is the light of men (John 1:4) and there are no shifting shadows or darkness in Him (James 1:17; 1 John 1:5).

The Holy Spirit guides us into all truth, revealing to us the "Star of Wonder"—the truth that leads us to the true Light. Jesus is "Immanuel—God with us." We do not fear the darkness, because we have seen and know Him who is light, and we have yielded ourselves to His mighty and loving care.

> *...God needs only one Word to perfectly communicate the depth and mystery, the passion and the overwhelming grace of who He is. By that Word, Light became a living being....In Him, Life came to life; all that God is came to us....*
>
> —Michael Card, *Immanuel*

Worship with your heart fully yielded; worship the King who sits on a throne called "Mercy." Your King has grace, mercy, and delight to pour over you; He has become man and walked among us and dispelled the darkness of our foolish, independent ways. He will lead you where miracles never cease and light leads you from glory to glory.

Our broken world is filled with men and women caught up in greed and lust for power and influence, and they will grasp at any opportunity to gain advantage and prominence, regardless of cost. Jesus, although worthy of pre-eminence and glory in the world of men, did not insist on receiving anything for Himself, and He bids us to live that same way. We are invited to bow in humility, with love and gratitude for His goodness and faithfulness. His promises are glorious and His grace is a gift, available to all who believe.

The Lord has spoken to us in His Word, telling us that His desire is for all people, all nations, to come before His presence, where we learn His ways and walk in His paths. We will fellowship with Him, love Him with all our hearts, and walk in His light (Isaiah 2:1-5; John 14:3, 17:24; Revelation 21:1-4; Ephesians 1:17-23). Jesus is the Bright and Morning Star—our Star of Wonder—and we are honored to respond and offer ourselves before Him, like the gifts the wise men set before Jesus, like Mary who trusted and said to the angel "*...let it be to me according to your word.*" We have the honor to surrender everything, for He alone is worthy.

10

Our Lives Declare His Glory

Our God is so great, His majesty so astonishing, that we sometimes find it difficult to offer an exclamation of worship worthy of Him, and our prayers of surrender often feel forced and limp. But, throughout the centuries, millions of people have found consolation and strength and expression for their joys, their sorrows, their confusions, their victories and defeats by reading from the songbook of the Scriptures. There are no human emotions or circumstances that are not addressed in the Psalms.

We also find powerful declarations of trust, and great exclamations of the wonder we find in our God such as,

> *The heavens declare the glory of God,*
> *and the sky above proclaims his handiwork.*
> *Day to day pours out speech,*
> *and night to night reveals knowledge.*
> *There is no speech, nor are there words,*
> *whose voice is not heard.*
> *Their voice goes out through all the earth,*
> *and their words to the end of the world*
> (Psalm 19:1-4).

Declarations do not need to only consist of audible speech; they can be displayed with beauty through the wonders of creation, or revealed in power by events in nature, or demonstrated in the grand sweep of history. Everywhere we look, if we have eyes to perceive, we find demonstrations of the Lord's glory and majesty. Our lives, also, can declare, demonstrate, and pour forth speech without us ever using words.

As we walk in alignment and obedience to God's ways and wisdom, we become a living demonstration of the glory of God for people around us to see. Our lives exhibit the message of peace, love, and joy. In unity and oneness of spirit with Christ, the sons and daughters of God are revealed to heaven and earth (we will examine this further in chapter thirty-two). As you heed God's counsel in your life, you are refreshed. You find yourself delighting more and more in fellowship with the Holy Spirit, and you find yourself more attuned to His leading, hearing His voice with increased discernment. You become a living example of Jesus—a "letter" written by Him that people are able to read, if they have eyes to see (2 Corinthians 3:2-3).

You realize that His commandments are not burdensome, but health- and life-giving, and it is your joy to discover that intimacy with Him creates within you a greater passion for obedience and true holiness. Living in this way, which before might seem lofty and unobtainable becomes easy—simple and light—giving you joy.

> *The law of the LORD is perfect,*
> *reviving the soul;*
> *the testimony of the LORD is sure,*
> *making wise the simple;*
> *the precepts of the LORD are right,*
> *rejoicing the heart;*
> *the commandment of the LORD is pure,*
> *enlightening the eyes;*
> *the fear of the LORD is clean,*
> *enduring forever;*
> *the just decrees of the LORD are true,*
> *and righteous altogether* (Psalm 19:7-9).

Surrendering to the will of God and submitting your entire life to His instruction is like laying up treasure for yourself as you are created to be a costly jewel belonging to Him (Malachi 3:17). You are daily placing a crown of wisdom on your head as you take on the mind of Christ, which gives great benefit to you, to your family, and to people in your life who will heed your counsel.

Proverbs speaks of receiving and heeding instruction, which produces wisdom. Abraham listened to and believed God's voice and his faith—which the Father considered obedience—became a blessing to all the nations of the earth.[3]

Ask the Holy Spirit for grace to obey as He teaches you. You will rejoice in the benefits that His wisdom produces, and your life will display the glory of God

[3] W.E. Vine, Merrill F. Unger & William White, Jr., *An Expository Dictionary of Biblical Words* (Nashville: Thomas Nelson, Inc., 1984), 176.

11

You Are of Great Value

"Consider the lilies, how they grow: they neither toil nor spin, yet I tell you, even Solomon in all his glory was not arrayed like one of these. But if God so clothes the grass, which is alive in the field today, and tomorrow is thrown into the oven, how much more will he clothe you, O you of little faith" (Luke 12:27-28).

The world is filled with the artistry of our Lord. There is profound beauty in the colors of fall leaves and the cottony blossoms of spring; in snow-capped crags of mountain peaks; in the waves and patterns created by the wind rippling across desert sand; in expansive fields of emerald dotted with golden-haired blossoms refreshed under summer rain. God's artistry in creation overwhelms our senses. He has clothed the earth in radiant beauty and glorious splendor, yet His Word says that He has *"all the more clothed us."*

As you continue to yield to the work of the Spirit in your life, you will experience a greater awakening to the reality of your personal value and to the greatness of God's love for you. This awakening will be like receiving royal robes and white linens that will clothe you anew. When God looks upon you, He sees such splendor and beauty—far more than even the most beautiful setting on Earth. He recognizes His divine artistry in you—His creation.

You are of such great value that there is no need to fear or fret about earthly things. You are an eternal being who has been wrapped in heavenly love that will never be removed. Grace clothes you in robes of righteousness as you have yielded to salvation's covering. You are the inheritance and joy of Jesus; you are His radiant bride whom He cherishes and protects. He cares for your every need.

When I (Kathi) was a teenager my life was very difficult. I felt that I had no value or worth beyond pleasing others by giving them what they wanted from me. During this time, a youth leader at my high school began to talk to me about having a relationship with Jesus. I was surprised and somewhat intrigued; I had never heard of such a thing. An acquaintance gave me an album by the Christian music artist Keith Green. Though I did not yet know Jesus, I found myself listening to one particular song named "When I Hear the Praises Start" over and over. The words of the song would cause me to weep, and I would experience a feeling I was not able to comprehend; it was like being washed clean. I felt as if the lyrics clothed me and covered me in worth and great value.

Even though I had no idea what Keith Green meant when he sang about "resting in faith," something deep inside me recognized the tender power of a God who would assure me that He was able to make me clean and cause me to be holy. I wanted to rest in the loving arms of God who would save and protect me. I just had no idea how to do that; and I did not think God would want me, even though my heart longed to be pure and free. (If you have never heard the song, we encourage you to find it and listen to it.)

A few years after I came to know the Lord, I realized how much Keith's lyrics brought to mind the words of Jesus in Luke 12:

> *"Consider how the wild flowers grow. They do not labor or spin. Yet I tell you, not even Solomon in all his splendor was dressed like one of these. If that is how God clothes the grass of the field, which is here today, and tomorrow is thrown into the fire, how much more will he clothe you..."* (Luke 12:27-28).

Now, whenever I listen to Keith Green's song, it takes me back to the days in my youth when the words began to cover my shame and nakedness, leading me to the greatest and purest love I've ever known. No matter how the years have passed, what mistakes I have made, how often I have fallen down or fallen short, nothing that I do can strip me of His love and grace. The garments of salvation never become tattered or soiled, dull or aged; but they remain beautiful—the expression of His faithfulness and mercy upon me each day.

> *The steadfast love of the Lord never ceases;*
> *his mercies never come to an end;*
> *they are new every morning;*
> *great is your faithfulness*
> (Lamentations 3:22-23).

Yielding in surrender to His goodness and love is rekindling first love. It is walking in trust, allowing Him to pour out on us His goodness and kindness. The Spirit of God reminds us of the greatness of His love toward us: the people He created and Jesus gave His life to redeem from every nation, tribe, people, and language (Revelation 7:9). We do not need to worry, strive, or weep, for we are His children; we are His bride. We have been clothed in the splendor of His love and are held by the arms of a God who will never let us go. There is nothing we have done that will permanently stain what He has made clean, and there is nothing that we can do to separate ourselves from His great love. The greater our yielding, the greater His beauty is displayed in our lives.

> *Why do you say, O Jacob, and speak, O Israel,*
> *"My way is hidden from the Lord,*
> *and my right is disregarded by my God"?*
> *Have you not known? Have you not heard?*
> *The Lord is the everlasting God,*
> *the Creator of the ends of the earth.*
> *He does not faint or grow weary;*
> *his understanding is unsearchable.*
> *He gives power to the faint,*
> *and to him who has no might he increases strength.*

Even youths shall faint and be weary,
and young men shall fall exhausted;
but they who wait for the Lord *shall renew their strength;*
they shall mount up with wings like eagles;
they shall run and not be weary;
they shall walk and not faint
(Isaiah 40:27-31)

12

Receiving Wisdom

Our world is in desperate need of wisdom. The nations of the world rage against each other, and almost everywhere you look there is civil and social disruption. Often, you will hear people discuss the need for more "education," and certainly that is helpful; but what we need, above all else, is wisdom that comes from our Creator, which He releases to those who trust Him, who have humble and teachable hearts.

It is overwhelming to recognize the goodness and grace God is pouring out on us. A transformation is taking place that allows us to soar upon the winds of the Spirit. The mercy of God is freeing us from fear and false beliefs that have lain heavy on our hearts and minds, crushing us under the oppressive patterns of the world rather than releasing us in the freedom found in the love of the Father.

Now the Spirit is pleased to give us wisdom and instructions that we need for our personal lives as well as wisdom for the life of His corporate body in the days ahead.

Scripture is the plumb line of all wisdom. The Word of God is our infallible, authoritative, complete guide for how we are to live our lives in every aspect. His Word is truth; it does not simply *contain* truth, it is truth (or perhaps more accurately, it is the truth about the Truth). The Bible is totally sufficient for all training in righteousness, as we read and meditate with humble hearts and rely on the Holy Spirit to bring revelation and understanding. In His mercy He reveals His ways and aligns our lives with

His statutes, giving us corporate as well as individual authority. Greater authority is released as we move into greater alignment.

> ***Alignment is an order that allows for everyone to have his or her own place—for everyone to function, for everyone to bear fruit. Alignment is an order based on intimacy and submission. It starts with Yeshua and the Father and extends into every possible group where two or more people are gathered together for a common purpose.***
> **—Asher Intrater, *Alignment***

We read in Zechariah 3 that after the LORD rebuked Satan and changed Joshua's filthy garments, He then gave him instructions of how to live and renewed his understanding of the importance and position of the priesthood. These instructions were the bridge between iniquities of the past—both his and the people he represented—and the position of purity, righteousness, and authority for the days ahead.

> *"This is what the LORD of Heaven's Armies says: If you follow my ways and carefully serve me, then you will be given authority over my Temple and its courtyards. I will let you walk among these others standing here"* (Zechariah 3:7, NLT).

As we continue to yield our will and our ways to the Lord, He is faithful to reveal His ways and His wisdom that we need to walk forward. We must remember that His ways are not our ways, and His thoughts are not our thoughts. However, He will reveal His counsel to His people who seek to know Him. He will not be manipulated by our desires or our "good ideas"; His statutes will not fit into the patterns of the world or our natural thinking. His wisdom is filled with mysteries that will take you higher than you could have ever imagined.

> *"Call to me and I will answer you, and will tell you great and hidden things that you have not known"* (Jeremiah 33:3).

It is exciting to realize that as we seek the Lord in intimacy, He shares "great and hidden things"—remarkable secrets—that grants us new realms of authority, favor, and wisdom for the days to come. This is meant to bring His people into greater unity with each other as we draw closer to Him in love. Obedience to His statutes positions His people in favor and authority that brings breakthrough. This is not only for personal breakthrough, but it also opens a way for our families and those around us to experience increased breakthrough. Yielding our will for the sake of alignment with the King and His Kingdom helps effect change upon cities and nations. May His Kingdom come and will be done on earth as it is in heaven!

Here are amazing promises the Lord told Israel they would receive if they walked in obedience. They are worth our study and prayerful consideration.

> *"If you walk in my statutes and observe my commandments and do them, then I will give you your rains in their season, and the land shall yield its increase, and the trees of the field shall yield their fruit. Your threshing shall last to the time of the grape harvest, and the grape harvest shall last to the time for sowing. And you shall eat your bread to the full and dwell in your land securely. I will give peace in the land, and you shall lie down, and none shall make you afraid. And I will remove harmful beasts from the land, and the sword shall not go through your land. You shall chase your enemies, and they shall fall before you by the sword. Five of you shall chase a hundred, and a hundred of you shall chase ten thousand, and your enemies shall fall before you by the sword. I will turn to you and make you fruitful and multiply you and will confirm my covenant with you. You shall eat old store long kept, and you shall clear out the old to make way for the new. I will make my dwelling among you, and my soul shall not abhor you. And I will walk among you and will be your God, and you shall be my people. I am the Lord your God, who brought you out of the land of Egypt, that you should not be their slaves. And I have broken the bars of your yoke and made you walk erect"* (Leviticus 26:3-13).

Our Father is serious about obedience, because He knows the blessing and flourishing that is released for all creation when we obey. Jesus is our obedience and our glorious High Priest, who completely fulfilled all righteousness. In Him, we have access to all the fullness of God. The rich promises in Scripture are not simply nice, poetic words; they are guarantees from our faithful God! They are words that we can stake our lives upon as we live in accordance with His Word and His ways.

Our "Yes" to God

Our lives have been a series of responding "yes" to God regarding a lot of different things He's placed in our paths.

A few years ago we found ourselves being a little battle-fatigued after not seeing the fruit we thought we would see from one of those risky "yeses." It can be easier to say yes to the Lord regarding something that you have a good prior history with, however when it comes to saying yes again to something that hasn't worked out the way you were hoping, it can be quite hard to trust once more.

It was just such an occurrence when the Lord asked us to invest our lives and resources into making another album. We knew that there was a sound and a message in us that needed to be released through song, but we also knew that we didn't have any physical means to make that happen. Combine this with the fact that we weren't sure of our emotional capacity to lay ourselves out there again, after the seeming failure of our previous venture into this area. But even with all the limitations facing us, we decided to proceed with our big YES to God.

He gave us wisdom, guidance, and resources throughout the entire process. We felt that we were not to look at the current limitations before us, but invest extravagantly into this particular assignment. As with many financial shortcomings, we often try to work out the solution ourselves. For us, this was to consider crowd funding as a way to pay the seventy-five thousand dollars that it would take to produce the album. As we were praying about this option, we both felt a strong "no" from the Lord. We felt that He wanted to demonstrate His provision, not by natural means which could be explained away, but by the miracle of a supernatural multiplication of what He had already placed into our hands. The next several months, as we worked on the album, we were amazed as God's provision was released in many miraculous and unexpected ways. He truly multiplies our "loaves and fishes."

We planned a party for the night of our album release, but a huge storm roared into town, so a lot of people weren't able to come and celebrate with us. As I was sat during the party, observing just a few friends and family around us, the enemy tried to take advantage of the situation and began spewing lies of failure once again. For a moment, I considered partnering with the fear, but I stood up and refused to enter into an agreement with those lies. We had a great evening of talking and worshipping together, and close to end of the evening we got a text from our producer with a screen shot of the latest album charts, and our album debuted in between "This is Not a Test" by tobyMac and before "Welcome to the New" by MercyMe. It was a surreal moment to see our names on the same chart with performers who have had a tremendous amount of success in the music business. Since that time, we saw God come through with His provision for the album, and we have had the honor to release our music to many churches and conferences, as well as seeing our music being engaged with internationally.

The results of our yes to God often looks a lot different than what we thought it would, but we can have the confidence to know that whatever it looks like, it will be good.

~Ty Bottler

13

The Sound of His Answer

Ascribe to the Lord, *O heavenly beings,*
ascribe to the Lord *glory and strength.*
Ascribe to the Lord *the glory due his name;*
worship the Lord *in the splendor of holiness*
(Psalm 29:1-2).

We are grateful for the wonderful things the Lord has done for us. We have recognized the lies we have believed; the accusations against us have been dealt with; we understand our value to our Lord and we rejoice as we understand more deeply the beauty and power of our union with our Creator, the Lover of our lives. We receive His wisdom and counsel and strength to overcome our enemies and restore righteousness in our spheres of influence. He truly is the light in our darkness and He forges a pathway through the tangled wilderness of confusion and trouble. As we continue in this journey of yielding, we worship ADONAI and give Him the honor that He deserves, for He has done great things for us and we are filled with joy!

When God's people cry out Him, He is faithful to answer. Psalm 29 is a powerful declaration of worship, and it reveals profound truth about the sound of God's voice. As we worship Him with songs of praise and shouts of "Glory!" He responds with power and the sound of His voice,

The voice of the Lord *is powerful;*

the voice of the Lord is majestic.
The voice of the Lord splits the mighty cedars;
the Lord shatters the cedars of Lebanon.
He makes Lebanon's mountains skip like a calf;
he makes Mount Hermon leap like a young wild ox.
The voice of the Lord strikes with bolts of lightning.
The voice of the Lord makes the barren wilderness
quake;
the Lord shakes the wilderness of Kadesh.
The voice of the Lord twists mighty oaks
and strips the forests bare.
In his Temple everyone shouts, "Glory!"
(Psalm 29:4-9, NLT).

God's voice is incredible, fearful, powerful, awe-inspiring. We have looked at the way God's voice rebuked the accuser. His voice shatters the mountains that stand in your way; His voice declares innocence over your life; His voice proclaims breakthrough for your needs; His voice speaks promises and causes them to be fulfilled. As we release our voices in worship, He releases His voice over us and all circumstances shift that need to be shifted. The power of praise and the power of the voice of the Lord join together to break curses of spiritual barrenness and to restore blessings of fruitfulness in His people.

The Lord sat enthroned at the Flood,
And the Lord sits as King forever.
The Lord will give strength to His people;
the Lord will bless His people with peace
(Psalm 29:10-11, NLT).

He is King! He rules over all creation and it is He alone who gives strength and peace to those who put their trust in Him. Psalm 29 is a breathtaking account of the voice of our Father; and in many other places the Bible speaks of the magnificence of His voice that is beyond our comprehension, performing wonders.

One day, as I (Kathi) was praying, I was surprised to hear a roaring sound that seemed filled with fierce passion. It was powerful, like turbulent ocean waves crashing against a wall, like rolling thunder on a stormy night. I asked the Spirit what the sound was and He answered, *"It is the sound of the Father arising to answer the cries of distress that come from His children."* Then I began to hear the words from Psalm 18:

> *The Lord also thundered in the heavens,*
> *and the Most High uttered his voice,*
> *hailstones and coals of fire.*
> *And he sent out his arrows and scattered them;*
> *he flashed forth lightnings and routed them.*
> *Then the channels of the sea were seen,*
> *and the foundations of the world were laid bare*
> *at your rebuke, O Lord,*
> *at the blast of the breath of your nostrils*
> (Psalm 18:13-15).

Satan rages against the mighty work of grace in your life, because he only understands condemnation and penalty; grace is a sound that he cannot identify, interpret, or understand. If you have been experiencing warfare against your life or your family during this time then realize the Father is arising to answer your cry and once again rebuke the enemy,

> *And the Lord said to satan, "The Lord rebuke you, O satan! The Lord who has chosen Jerusalem rebuke you! Is not this a brand plucked from the fire?"* (Zechariah 3:2).

When satan rages and hell attempts to assault us, we call out to our Father, and He answers with His power; by the words of His mouth, He Himself rebukes and destroys the works of darkness. The words from His lips are unimaginably powerful, performing everything He sends them to accomplish. Isaiah received a revelation of God dealing with the enemies of Israel, as He displaces and destroys wickedness with His very breath:

Behold, the name of the LORD comes from afar,
burning with his anger, and in thick rising smoke;
his lips are full of fury,
and his tongue is like a devouring fire;
his breath is like an overflowing stream
that reaches up to the neck;
to sift the nations with the sieve of destruction...
And the LORD will cause his majestic voice to be heard
and the descending blow of his arm to be seen,
in furious anger and a flame of devouring fire,
with a cloudburst and storm and hailstones
(Isaiah 30:27-28, 30).

When you yield to Him each day you are supernaturally changed and renewed in mind and spirit, and you realize how powerful your Father is as He deals with your accuser. This terrifies the enemy and he cannot understand how this can happen, because you are not striving or working for it. Your yielding provokes the jealous love of God, and He arises with a sound that releases protection and power to defend you.

In my distress I called upon the LORD;
to my God I cried for help.
From his temple he heard my voice,
and my cry to him reached his ears.
Then the earth reeled and rocked;
the foundations also of the mountains trembled
and quaked, because he was angry.
Smoke went up from his nostrils,
and devouring fire from his mouth;
glowing coals flamed forth from him.
He bowed the heavens and came down;
thick darkness was under his feet.
He rode on a cherub and flew;
he came swiftly on the wings of the wind
(Psalm 18:6-10).

The Lord is your defender, protector, and provider. He is a mighty shield around you (Psalm 3:3) surrounding you with favor as you trust Him (Psalm 5:11-12). As you stand in the presence of Jesus as part of the great company of yielded ones—allowing this great work of grace to transform you—He defends you, watching over the work of His hands. He guards you in all your ways. Read Psalm 18:30-32, 46.

> *This God—his way is perfect;*
> *the word of the LORD proves true;*
> *he is a shield for all those who take refuge in him.*
> *For who is God, but the LORD?*
> *And who is a rock, except our God?—*
> *the God who equipped me with strength*
> *and made my way blameless*
> *The LORD lives, and blessed be my rock,*
> *and exalted be the God of my salvation—*

We encourage you to read both Psalms 18 and 29, and meditate on the truths presented there. Then enter into thanksgiving and praise for who He is and all that He has done.

> ***No matter what view of God we have, it's not big enough.***
> —MIKE ERRE, ***Astonished***

14

I Will Not Fear

The great and mighty Lord, the Creator of all things, is our protector, our shield, our defender. The LORD Almighty is our Rock, the awesome Warrior-King who vanquishes every enemy and whose voice causes all hell to tremble; yet this infinite one is our gentle Father!

Some people grow up with abusive, or neglectful, or disinterested fathers. This was never God's intention for fatherhood. A child should always be able to count on his or her father for nurture, love, and protection; should be comforted by a strong arm to pull the child close when trouble threatens: an arm so big that it shields every part of the little one.

> *He who dwells in the shelter of the Most High*
> *will abide in the shadow of the Almighty.*
> *I will say to the LORD, "My refuge and my fortress,*
> *my God, in whom I trust"* (Psalm 91:1-2).

Because this is our God, who loves us, we can declare, *"In Him I will trust!"* As we grow from childhood to adulthood, we become more independent and gradually take on the burdens that come with adult life. This is normal and natural, and though we must work hard and live as responsible men and women, we must not become independent from the care and counsel of our Father. We are fully dependent on Him for every good thing. Jesus instructed us to take only His light burden upon ourselves, trusting in His work in our lives, believing that He will direct us with perfect wisdom, knowing that He has a future and hope for us. We do not achieve the promises of this hope through our independent actions, but rather through trust and loving dependency.

As we read about the accomplishments of men and women of God in the Bible, we must realize that they were able to do these things only because they were yielded and surrendered to Him. Moses could not have delivered the Jews from the captivity of Egypt apart from being yielded to the sovereignty of God. Abraham had to yield to finally gain his son Isaac and become the father of everyone who would believe. Joshua and Caleb had to yield to find God's favor to enter and possess the Promised Land. The apostles had to yield to walk with Jesus and receive the astonishing, world-transforming power of the Holy Spirit. Mary had to yield to become the chosen woman who would be the mother of our Messiah. Every man and woman who surrenders to Jesus must yield fully to see their lives move from the mundane to the miraculous.

Heroes of the faith learned that yielding meant surrendering their will to obey the will of God. God often asks us to accomplish what seems impossible, but our first response and responsibility is to yield by saying "yes." Then He will lead us into even deeper surrender, allowing us to become fully dependent; as we do, we enter into a trust that shatters natural fears. We will not fear, because we dwell in the secret place, under the mighty arm of our God.

You will not fear the terror of the night,
nor the arrow that flies by day,
nor the pestilence that stalks in darkness,
nor the destruction that wastes at noonday.
A thousand may fall at your side,
ten thousand at your right hand,
but it will not come near you...
Because you have made the LORD your dwelling place—
the Most High, who is my refuge—

no evil shall be allowed to befall you,
no plague come near your tent.
For he will command his angels concerning you
to guard you in all your ways.
On their hands they will bear you up,
lest you strike your foot against a stone
(Psalm 91:5-12).

Just like that child drawn into safety by the strong arm, you too are fully shielded as he draws you near. To live outside the shadow of His wing is to be left vulnerable to the fierce battles and heavy burdens of life, but in the place of dependency we are set free to run and not be weary, to walk and not faint, and have our lives renewed daily.

This truth leads us back to Zechariah 3. Just as Joshua did nothing but stand, so we also posture ourselves in the quiet rest of trust and surrender, under God's protection. We allow His wing to become like the white linen that covers our nakedness and protects us in our battles.

We will not fear for He is our refuge! These are His words to us—we are honored and rescued; we are saved:

"Because he holds fast to me in love, I will deliver him;
I will protect him, because he knows my name.
When he calls to me, I will answer him;
I will be with him in trouble;
I will rescue him and honor him.
With long life I will satisfy him
and show him my salvation" (Psalm 91:14-16).

15

Peace on Earth, Goodwill to Men

When we know the love of our gracious Father, we understand the angel's proclamation to shepherds when Jesus was born. "Peace on earth, good will to men" is a declaration from the Creator of all things, revealing the longing and desire in His heart that all the earth, indeed, all His creation, would flourish under His loving care. He wants us to experience everything He created us to enjoy: peace, goodness, joy, adoration, and a love that brings *all things* together in beautiful unity. The longing within this declaration takes our breath away and causes our heart to race with a fresh revelation of His love for all that He has created.

But a pernicious lie has existed and been repeated almost as long as mankind has been on the earth. It began with the first couple accepting the whispered seductions of the serpent, who hissed that God was actually deceiving them; that their Creator was not "playing it straight." The twisting one placed doubts in their minds about the goodness and integrity of their kind Lord. Since that time, people believe the lie that God is not really for them; if He exists at all, He is an unconcerned and unknowable deity, flinging galaxies from His hands and listening for an occasional cry for help—to which He may (but probably won't) respond.

And many do not even believe in any god or existence of the supernatural. If they are not convinced atheists, they function as if they were, for they live their daily lives as if they were their own god, the "master of their fate and captain of their soul." They hope that they do enough good deeds to get into heaven (if there is one) after they die. The thought of a good Father who loves them and is devoted to caring for them sounds like unenlightened superstition, a childish fairy tale.

And it seems that we all, believer and unbeliever alike, must fight against the desire to have anything or anyone rule over us. Adam and Eve took their destiny into their own hands, and every one of us has been struggling through that battle ever since. We try to run our lives the way we think best, and when circumstances overwhelm and chaos upends us, we fear that God is not to be trusted, that He is not good and His loving-kindness is *not* everlasting.

Can you hear the cry of our faithful, passionate, merciful God? *"Oh, that none may perish but all would know the depth, height, and width of My love for the ones I died for."*

The mercy of God is stirred to intervene on behalf of those who have no ears to hear or eyes to see. Like Joshua the high priest who was a "brand plucked from the fire" or Paul on the road to Damascus who was apprehended by grace, can you feel the mercy of God reaching down to capture those who have been held captive by sin and death? God's desire is "peace on earth." His heart is filled with "goodwill to men." He groans, *"Oh, that none should perish!"*

The Lord's longing is not about right or wrong but rather it is the deep desire of a loving Father who wants His children to experience all the love and beauty that they were created for. Just as the prodigal son's father waited patiently for his return, the heavenly Father eagerly and tirelessly waits to embrace and restore those who have left His home and loving arms.

He desires that we yield to the longing and love that continually flows from His very heart. He has promised to forgive our sins and cleanse us. He has promised us peace, joy, and abundant life. Will we believe in His promises?

> *One of the greatest challenges of the spiritual life is to receive God's forgiveness. There is something in us humans that keeps us clinging to our sins and prevents us from letting God erase our past and offer us a completely new beginning. Sometimes it even seems as though I want to prove to God that my darkness*

> *is too great to overcome....Do I truly want to be so totally forgiven that a completely new way of living becomes possible? Do I want to break away from my deep-rooted rebellion against God and surrender myself so absolutely to God's love that a new person can emerge? Receiving forgiveness requires a total willingness to let God be God and do all the healing, restoring, and renewing.*
>
> —Henri J.M. Nouwen, *The Return of the Prodigal Son*

We can trust our Father. When circumstances promote a message of fear and we are tempted to despair, wondering why His promises and protection are delayed, we must go to the Scriptures, discover the truth and proclaim our trust, surrendering our lives once again to His care.

> *The Lord is not slow to fulfill his promise as some count slowness, but is patient toward you, not wishing that any should perish, but that all should reach repentance* (2 Peter 3:9).

Reject and renounce every lingering thought of unbelief that aligns you with doubt because God is not a man that he should lie. Though there is a thief that comes to kill, steal, and destroy (John 10:10a), we belong to our Advocate, the Redeemer who has purchased us with His own blood and who is the Keeper of promises. He fights for all of His children to live in abundant life (John 10:10b).

As you allow His Spirit to remove doubts from you, enter into His longing for His lost and straying sons and daughters who are still bound by lies, in captivity to the strongholds of sin and death. Call them to come; call the prodigals to return to the Father's house. Weep with Him for the ones that He weeps for. Call for them to set out on the road called "Mercy" that leads them home to the peace and goodness of their Father.

16

The God of Second Chances

To be saved is to be given a second chance. When Jesus paid the price for sin's penalty, drinking the cup of God's righteous judgment for all humanity's wickedness, it created the way for every person to receive a second chance through a full and complete pardon.

As we have studied the third chapter of Zechariah, we have discovered such an amazing illustration of God giving someone a second chance. Joshua's second chance was purely an act of grace. Joshua and the people of Israel had been soiled by iniquities and bombarded with accusations; and they were most likely accusations of things that were true. Joshua and the people needed a second chance!

God did what only He can do by rebuking satan and his taunting accusations. The enemy most likely had a solid case against Joshua based on his actual iniquities; but we must remember that the devil can bring accusation and even evidence, but he cannot condemn! God is the only true High Priest and Righteous Judge over every person who has ever lived. Even when our lives and actions give cause for accusation, and evidence of iniquity can be presented against us, we stand firm in the truth that **there is NO condemnation for those in Christ Jesus!** The price for all sin, for all time, was paid by the precious blood of

Jesus and He bore our iniquity in His body and nailed it to the cross. The Lord Jesus, the eternal Son of God, our Savior, paid the full price for our guilty verdict so that we can walk free.

> *There is therefore now no condemnation for those who are in Christ Jesus. For the law of the Spirit of life has set you free in Christ Jesus from the law of sin and death* (Romans 8:1-2).

So, just as Zechariah saw Joshua cleansed and clothed in new, clean garments, and saw him restored to his position and authority, in the same way Jesus has done that for everyone who accepts His ransom for their sin by believing and trusting in His finished work. We are not just forgiven from sin, as wonderful as that is; we are given a second chance to live in freedom from our sin and its power that leads to death. By grace, we have not only been saved, but we have been clothed in the righteousness of Jesus Christ. All the benefits of His righteousness are ours; we are not only free from penalty, we are also given the rewards of His righteousness. The Spirit of God now lives within us, causing us to walk in freedom from sin and continually granting us His wisdom, counsel, and power.

> *For God has done what the law, weakened by the flesh, could not do. By sending his own Son in the likeness of sinful flesh and for sin, he condemned sin in the flesh, in order that the righteous requirement of the law might be fulfilled in us, who walk not according to the flesh but according to the Spirit* (Romans 8:3-4).

Through Christ, you are now able to follow the instructions that come from God. God declared an end to sin's control over you! Though the enemy still loves to whisper thoughts that accuse us, tempting us to replay the memories of our failures and live in past regrets, we can reply to those taunting accusations with the same words that the LORD spoke to satan as he accused Joshua, *"The LORD rebuke you!"*

We declare his Name and let the enemy know that ADONAI

Himself rebukes every blasphemous accusation against each of us, who are the people of God. Those accusations are not in line with the Word of God. Boldly proclaim the wondrous truth of Romans 8:1 every time an accusation brings up guilt, regret, and dread: **There is therefore now no condemnation for those who are in Christ Jesus.**

The enemy wants us to come into agreement with accusation so that he can ensnare us into believing we have to pay a penalty that has already been paid for. Our condemnation is gone, the price has been paid, and sin's control has been broken over our lives. We are now the recipients of abundant and eternal life. We stand, clothed anew, in the white robes of the righteousness of Jesus. We have yielded to His gift of grace, to being cleansed by His blood; accepting the one who gave His all for our freedom.

Obedience to the Lord is necessary to move forward in maturity and authority, but it is the power of the Spirit within us that helps us to walk in God's ways. It is the oil of His Spirit that anoints us, making our steps pleasing to the Lord, and purifies us from all iniquities.

> *Then he said to me, "This [continuous supply of oil] is the word of the Lord to Zerubbabel [prince of Judah], saying, 'Not by might, nor by power, but by My Spirit [of whom the oil is a symbol],' says the Lord of hosts* (Zechariah 4:6, AMP).

The Holy Spirit and His presence in us is the pure oil that keeps our lamps burning, looking forward to the return of our Lord. Ask for the oil of the Spirit, which causes you to walk in purity and holiness. Ask Him to continue to reveal any dependency you may have on your own strength, and submit it to Him, asking instead for the strength of His Spirit. Walk by the Spirit and not by the flesh. He is your second chance!

Yielding to His Spirit

What a journey leaning in to yielding to His Spirit is. In honest reflection I would have to say that hearing God has been easier than surrendering to what I heard many times! And yet, the longer I have journeyed with God, the deeper ingrained in the core of my being is the truth that "God rewards those who diligently seek Him," and that to surrender to the whispers of heaven, is the greatest of honours. I've discovered, as many of us have, through the real circumstances of pursuing His presence that the pearl of great price is the most precious of gifts to attain and is worthy of any and all sacrifice. It costs full surrender to Him, which is ecstatically wonderful, and yet sometimes excruciatingly challenging as we yield to God's voice over our preferences. I've discovered time and time again, that half-surrender is not surrender at all.

The following are seemingly disconnected stories of surrender, but they all speak to the overarching truth that to love God is to serve God, and to serve God is to trust and yield our hearts to Him.

In one particular season I had specifically been pressing in for growth in hearing God's voice and as I prayed I heard God say, "11 a.m., The French Patisserie, yellow shirt." I wasn't entirely sure what it meant but I knew enough to know I didn't want to miss the opportunity to obey the Lord and follow his instructions, so I rushed to get ready and jumped in my car, drove there and literally ran to stand outside the cafe. I waited and searched for anyone with a yellow shirt. At 10.59 there had been every colour under the sun on people's clothing except yellow! I wondered had I got it wrong. Then as the time clicked to 11 a.m. a lady walked in with a yellow shirt and sat at a table right outside the café. She sat there for only a minute and by 11.01 a.m. she changed her mind and started walking off.

I excitedly (perhaps overly so) chased her down the street and proceeded to explain as best I could I'd been waiting for her as God had sent me to bless the lady in the yellow shirt, and I gave her an encouraging word, for which she seemed blessed. To be honest, I would have liked to see her blown away, tears and on-the-spot dramatic salvation, but the lady did seem thankful, if not surprised, and I trust seeds were planted that grew. I think I was the one more profoundly affected by this than her as I realised that the lady in the yellow shirt was exactly where God said she would be at the exact time, and only that time. Had I been late, or early, I would have missed this encounter. It spoke to me of God knowing exactly where people are, but also the importance of prioritising obeying WHEN God speaks and getting the timing right. Had I not been outside this cafe at exactly 11 a.m. I would have missed the moment God asked me to partner with Him. This spoke to me: I can miss God moments if I don't "turn aside" and yield my heart.

Another time, I was in a meeting worshipping as my husband Ben was leading and the glory was thick. I suddenly "heard" a violin playing and knew that there was only guitar, bass, and drums on the stage. I started looking around the room for someone playing a random violin and couldn't see anyone. The violin noise disappeared as quickly as I heard it and I started to wonder: had I heard it? *Then I would start worshipping and again I would hear this violin playing along with the worship. I began to look around the room again to see if anyone had a random instrument and as I did the violin noise disappeared. This happened several times, and each time I started wondering* am I really hearing this? *the noise disappeared.*

After a while, I started hearing a woodwind type sound join in, and after that, brass instruments. It was as clear as if they were on the stage playing with my husband; the sounds weren't in my head, they were loud and external to me and as clear as the rest of the worship. It sounded amazing, glorious even, but as I wondered was I really hearing this, or looking for where the additional worship was coming from, I would stop hearing it. Eventually I was hearing what sounded like a full orchestral band playing along with my husband as he worshipped. By this point, I knew I was hearing something angelic and precious. It truly was glorious, synchronized, and worshipping in full partnership with the rest of the worship. What stood out was that as my husband stopped one song, the angelic worship would pause as well, and as he started another song, they would join in the same song playing as if part of the band. The angels were indeed worshipping WITH us in this instance.

But later as I pondered why I kept hearing and then not hearing the heavenly sounds, I asked the Lord about it, and I heard, "every time you started doubting, you stopped hearing." Wow! How many times had my own doubt impacted my walk with the Lord and what I experienced with Him? "Lord I believe, but help my unbelief, even if it costs me" became a heartfelt prayer from then on.

I have since found myself in many circumstances and ministry situations that required leaps of faith upon hearing and sensing God's whispers. Sometimes (often) it required being prepared to look silly or foolish, or other times it cost my comfort or finances or supposed reputation to step into what I heard. Always it would seem there was a choice to surrender and yield to His voice, or doubt—did I really hear that? Many times I know I've "missed it", but I'm more determined than ever to not miss the heart-beat of heaven, in the timing of heaven, and surrender to His heart. My prayer is, "I'd rather doubt my doubt than miss turning aside and seeing the fire of God."

Recently I was in hospital in a protracted season of "medical challenges" that really took a toll on my body. I was walking around the hospital ward decreeing healing over the patient's rooms. I was determined that if the enemy had me in hospital then heaven would touch this place and people would be better off because I was there. I had drainage tubes coming from my body and a tube down my nose that made it really difficult, and somewhat painful, to breathe and swallow and sit, which honestly was a bit miserable. I was in pain, but thankful for a moment in different surroundings as I sat in lounge area.

I remember walking past one room and being particularly drawn to an old lady who looked skeletal and severely frail. I prayed as I walked past. As my husband and I sat in the lounge taking a moment away from my hospital bed to breathe and try and relax, another elderly lady patient was wheeled into the lounge. As I was about to leave, my husband pointed to the lady and I immediately knew I needed to take a moment and pray with her. I discovered she had recently been diagnosed with cancer and apart from one night when her daughter was born some fifty-odd years ago, had never spent a night away from her husband, and she made a comment that she "just wanted to go home."

She was frail, sick, hopeless, and hurting. Her eyes welled up as I prayed healing and blessed her and I walked off not seeing any change but knowing God's presence had touched her.

The rest of that day as I sat in my hospital bed I couldn't stop praying for this lady. Her name was Mary and over and over I thought of her and prayed for God to touch her. Thoughts of her weighted on my heart and I heard her comment over and over in my head that "she just wanted to go home." I was overcome as I realised that her deepest heart's cry was to go home and be with her husband, but really what her spirit was craving was a sense of "home" with the Lord. I knew without a miracle she would no doubt leave this earth soon and I was deeply aware she couldn't go home to Jesus as she didn't know Him. Suddenly I was compelled to get off my bed and find her. As I had seen her in the lounge I didn't know what room was hers but I knew her name was Mary. I started walking down one of the halls and felt drawn to the same room I had previously walked past and seen a skeletal lady I had prayed for. As I looked in the door, I saw Mary.

I walked straight up to her and said, "Mary, I've been thinking about you and praying for you all afternoon and God's sent me back to tell you that he loves you and that you don't have to do this alone as He wants to be with you and come into your life. It doesn't have to be this hard. God wants to help you. Would you like to have God in your heart, Mary? Would you like to ask God into your life?"

Mary bowed her head and sighed, then was silent and wouldn't look at me. I said again, "Mary, it's not as hard as you think. God wants to come into your life and help you and He's inviting you now to ask Him into your heart; would you like to do that?"

And again, she sighed a long sigh as if the weight of the decades past of fighting God were crashing in on her; then she looked at me and said, "Yes." In that moment, I prayed with Mary and led her in a brief moment of explaining the gospel and allowing the Holy Spirit to do what He does best—bring peace into her heart. We both had tears, and then a nurse walked in and I had to return to my bed. I cried the entire way back to my bed as I was overcome with the truth that this quite elderly lady had fought saying yes to God her entire life, and now was assured of eternity with her Father in heaven and His presence with her even now. I can't begin to communicate what joy this gave me. I may have been sick and in pain and trapped in hospital but Mary changed her eternal home! That's my kind of spiritual warfare!

Again, I was overcome. What if I hadn't gone back to pray with her? What if I had thought I already prayed and planted a seed; someone else can do the rest now? *What if I had just prayed for her from afar and thought* I'm too sick to go find her and pray again?

There are often many thoughts and lies and fears and doubts that come to tell us not to surrender to something God has asked of us. One such lie is that you're not together enough to be used of God. That's a big fat lie. I know I'm far from perfect, and have had medical challenges, and I've missed it many times. But my prayer is: "God, don't let 'me' get in the way of what you want to do. I give you me. I surrender to your whispers and give you me to use."

For most of us the very real battle of displacing doubt and learning to not just hear His voice, but obey Him, and do so promptly, is a continual growth journey. To determine not to miss a God-moment because of our thoughts of inadequacy or self-disqualification, but instead trust that if He asks us, it's us He wants, is half the battle. Daily we're invited to choose to surrender again and again. Many are called but few are chosen simply because few choose to say yes and surrender even when it costs.

My mother died suddenly from an aggressive onset of cancer, even though we had been praying and believing for her healing. After she died, we immediately began praying for resurrection as well; we had full faith for her healing and for her resurrection. My parents had recently seen a young girl resurrected from the dead and healed in their ministry in India, along with multitudes of salvations and healing in their twenty-plus years of ministry there. So after my mother's precious passing into eternity I became hurt, disappointed, and started to doubt if I could trust God. This didn't happen suddenly but over many months my usual passion and hunger after Him started to grow cold. Eventually in worship one day, I clearly heard the Lord say to me, "Will you still trust Me?"

What deeply impacted me was I heard the emotion in the Lord's words to my heart, and I knew in an instant that I had a choice to make. The Father was impacted deeply by my pain, and equally connected in heart to my freedom to choose or not choose Him. This broke my heart. My trying to understand had become an idol in my heart that brought only further pain and now distrust toward God. In a flash I knew that I needed to surrender my "right" or desire to understand before I would trust. Right there in that moment, I surrendered my heart all over again and tearfully surrendered my pain and disappointment to the Lord, choosing to trust even where I didn't fully understand. I placed my heart on the altar and chose "yes" again in the midst of pain, surrendering to my God and saying "I trust you Father, even where I don't see or understand or where it hurts."

I didn't stop missing my Mum, but God was faithful and my heart came back alive: my passion, joy, and hope returned. I've since had many dreams of my Mum speaking to me, even hugging me. I consider these precious gifts from God. I know I will see her again, and until then, I will use my life to release heaven on earth, and my prayer is that I will choose to surrender my heart every day to Him, especially when I don't fully understand.

I've seen so many things: supernatural amazing wonders, miracles, healings, and astounding impossible circumstances shift; but still to this day the greatest thing I've seen is the wonder of a broken, lost soul find healing and heart connection with God. And what I've discovered along the way is that God desires this far more than me. As I surrender to Him, He WILL use me to bring heaven to earth. In every circumstance there is an invitation to say yes to His promptings and leading and surrender to Him. It almost always costs something of me to choose this; but that is the pearl of great price. The reward of blessing the Father's heart is worth every cost.

~Jodie Hughes

SECTION THREE

Clothed in New Garments

Zechariah 3:5

Then I said, "They should also place a clean turban on his head." So they put a clean priestly turban on his head and dressed him in new clothes while the angel of the Lord stood by.

The LORD will renew your mind and place the mind of Christ upon you as a clean "priestly turban" that is recognized by both angels and demons. New garments have been placed upon you for this new day. Father speaks His words over you, "Behold, I make all things new" (Revelation 21:5). We cling to the truth that we are clothed in the righteousness of Christ and receive His incomparable riches.

We come fully dependent upon His mercy and love to renew our minds and wash our garments so our lives are free from conformity to the patterns of the world. Israel's priests were to minister to the LORD and represent the people before Him. Because of Jesus, we can receive, with grateful hearts, the rich robes that only priests of the Lord can wear. We not only present ourselves, but we also carry before Him the lives of those we love for whom He died.

God is asking us to yield to His Spirit in order to leave the old behind. We are in a new season, and are being made ready for the new. Though we've never been this way before, and do not know what the "new" will look like, we put our trust in the One who knows the end from the beginning and prepares us for the days ahead.

17

Grace Sufficient

"...a brand plucked from the fire" (Zechariah 3:2).

Just like Joshua the high priest, the Spirit of the Lord has plucked us from the fire; from the penalty of sin and death through the blood of Jesus.

There is a deep longing in every believer to have Him come and pluck their loved ones, their cities, and their nations from the fires of turmoil and violence, the fires of poverty and disease, the fires of darkness and sin. This longing finds voice in the cries of the Psalms and the complaints of the Prophets. It has been a longing of the faithful from the beginning even as we weep, knowing there must be something more—an answer to the pain and suffering we see around us. The ache is a longing for rescue that is fully obtainable as we confidently access the blood that speaks a better word.

> *You have come to Jesus, the one who mediates the new covenant between God and people, and to the sprinkled blood, which speaks of forgiveness instead of crying out for vengeance like the blood of Abel* (Hebrews 12:24).

It is the deep longing of God Himself that your loved ones and people from all nations be washed from the soot and stain and defilement of sin. He longs to remove the odor of death and decay; replacing it with the sweet fragrance of salvation. His body was broken and His blood was shed for the redemption of all things. Now you can stand on behalf of people and nations in the righteousness of Jesus Christ, and plead the blood of the Lamb over all.

> *But when Christ came as high priest of the good things that are now already here, he went through the greater and more perfect tabernacle that is not made with human hands, that is to say, is not a part of this creation. He did not enter by means of the blood of goats and calves; but he entered the Most Holy Place once for all by his own blood, thus obtaining eternal redemption* (Hebrews 9:11-12).

> *...by the open statement of the truth we would commend ourselves to everyone's conscience in the sight of God. And even if our gospel is veiled, it is veiled to those who are perishing. In their case the god of this world has blinded the minds of the unbelievers, to keep them from seeing the light of the gospel of the glory of Christ, who is the image of God. For what we proclaim is not ourselves, but Jesus Christ as Lord, with ourselves as your servants for Jesus' sake. For God, who said, "Let light shine out of darkness," has shone in our hearts to give the light of the knowledge of the glory of God in Jesus Christ* (2 Corinthians 4:2-6).

We have been rescued from the dominion of darkness and transferred into the kingdom and dominion of Jesus Christ where, through this blood, we have authority as sons and daughters.

> *Both in our own lives, then, and in the church's mission it is only the cross of Christ by which Satan has been defeated, which can prevail against him. It is still true today that 'they overcame him by the blood of the Lamb and by the word of their testimony; they did not love their lives so much as to shrink from death' (Rev. 12:11). Uncompromising witness to Christ is essential. So is the willingness, if necessary, to lay down our lives for his sake. But indispensible to both is the content of our faith and message, namely the objective, decisive victory of the Lamb over*

> *all the power of darkness, which he won when he shed his blood on the cross.*
> —JOHN R.W. STOTT, *The Cross of Christ*

Condemnation, guilt, torment, and every demonic assignment must flee when the blood of Jesus is applied.

> *For it pleased the Father that in Him all the fullness should dwell, and by Him to reconcile all things to Himself, by Him, whether things on earth or things in heaven, having made peace through the blood of His cross. And you, who once were alienated and enemies in your mind by wicked works, yet now He has reconciled in the body of His flesh through death, to present you holy, and blameless, and above reproach in His sight....* (Colossians 1:19-22).

We are free from bondage and torment, and free from the frantic striving of our own self-effort, because by the sacrifice of our Savior, we have been reconciled, made blameless, and we now can rest in His finished work.

> ***Grace is sufficient, even though we huff and puff with all our might to try to find something or someone it cannot cover. Grace is enough.***
> —BRENNAN MANNING, *All Is Grace*

The writer of Hebrews tells us that we have received a genuine rest and that we can cease from all works of our own hands (Hebrews 3:9-10). Jesus was fully God and fully man, and because He took our place, our pardon is complete and we have total access into the presence of our Father.

> *...with His own blood He entered the Most Holy Place once for all, having obtained eternal redemption. For if the blood of bulls and goats and the ashes of a heifer, sprinkling the*

> *unclean, sanctifies for the purifying of the flesh, how much more shall the blood of Christ, who through the eternal Spirit offered Himself without spot to God, cleanse your conscience from dead works to serve the living God?* (Hebrews 9:12-14).

Because we are completely free and totally accepted, the hiss of the accuser is now replaced with the kind voice of our Savior who calls out,

> *"Come to me, all you who are weary and burdened, and I will give you rest. Take my yoke upon you and learn from me, for I am gentle and humble in heart, and you will find rest for your souls. For my yoke is easy and my burden is light"* (Matthew 11:28-30).

Let Him carry your life, the lives of your loved ones, and the destiny of the land that you dwell in. Your responsibility is to trust and pray and plead the precious blood of Jesus over your life and all that you love, for the power of His blood is unending. Yield to the yoke that is easy and light which provides rest for your soul. He took all the world's wickedness and brokenness upon Himself, and His sacrifice is more than sufficient for us all.

> *...the mountain of God's grace rises sheer from the ocean of Emmanuel's suffering and sorrow. And they measure the same.*
> —R.A. Finlayson, *The Cross in the Experience of Our Lord*

18

God Purifies What the Enemy Has Defiled

Humility is a powerful virtue, one that is far more admired and spoken of than actually practiced.

We can often find ourselves chafing even as we seek humility, because God has a way of producing it in us through means we would rather not endure. It is wonderful to meditate on the call to oneness with Jesus and have our hearts enflamed with His love and majesty. We are excited by the thoughts of God pouring out miracles in us and through us. But, often just as we feel we are making great headway, something in life comes along and seems to derail us. It can even be something as simple as a minor disagreement, and suddenly we realize we still have many lessons to learn as we grow in becoming more like our Master. We are well-advised to submit to the process of humbling ourselves before God and other people, and to facing our own inability to save ourselves

We have considered the powerful story in Zechariah 3 of God's miraculous grace to save a man defiled by his own iniquities. The more we consider how wonderful that is, the more we are keenly aware of the continual work of grace at work in the lives of God's sons and daughters. His kindness and cleansing should not cause us to be puffed up in arrogance, thanking God that we are "not like other men"; instead, we should worship in gratitude for His marvelous mercy.

When we stand before the Father, fully clothed in the purity and righteousness of Jesus, we are continually transformed in our souls— our minds, character, thoughts, and feelings. As our minds are renewed, we grow in understanding of the mind of Christ; and as that happens our belief systems become aligned with truth, and we find ourselves more obedient to His commands as we do "what we sense the Father doing."

As God renews our minds, we are not only aware of our need to walk before the Lord in humility, but we also understand that, because of what our great High Priest has accomplished for us, we have been sanctified and made kings and priests before our Lord. We live by, and in, the grace of God. By grace we have been clothed with a righteousness not earned or obtained by the flesh but freely received by the Spirit. As the old, filthy garments have been removed, we have been set free from guilt and shame. Condemnation has no place within the gift of grace. Grace is always at work, renewing and purifying our souls from all the patterns of this world that we once lived in.

If you have ever lived in a region that has snow in the winter, you have probably stood and marveled at the beauty of snow falling upon an open field lined by leafless trees. As the snow drifts down it begins to cover the branches of each tree and the soil below, clothing the entire landscape in pure white. This is a gradual transformation that the land did nothing to accomplish; the trees and the soil merely received the pure, white garment that was given from above to clothe it from the nakedness of winter's bareness.

Joshua merely stood and received new garments—the pure white linen of priesthood—just as land receives the white covering of winter snow. This is a description of us, His people. We are changed from glory to glory as we are becoming—both collectively as well as individually—a pure bride for our awesome King. John the beloved was allowed to see a portion of our glorious destiny:

> *And I heard, as it were, the voice of a great multitude, as the sound of many waters and as the sound of mighty thunderings, saying, "Alleluia! For the Lord God Omnipotent reigns! Let us be glad and rejoice and give Him glory, for the marriage of the Lamb has come, and His wife has made herself ready." And to her it was granted to be arrayed in fine linen,*

> *clean and bright, for the fine linen is the righteous acts of the saints* (Revelation 19:6-8).

The father of lies is relentless in his desire to replay and remind God's people of their past iniquities, hoping to provoke them to wrap themselves once again in the old, filthy garments they used to wear. The enemy seeks to keep souls weakened by guilt and sickened by defilement, so that the light of Christ's redemption will be hidden behind shame and condemnation.

The definition of defilement is *"the act of defiling, or the state of being defiled; foulness; dirtiness; uncleanness. Corruption of morals, principles or character; impurity; pollution by sin."*[4] Jesus has clothed us in fine garments and removed our sins as far as the east is from the west. His grace and righteousness has set His people free from all iniquity and pollution by the enemy's defilement.

We are changed "from glory to glory" (2 Corinthians 3:18) as we continue to put on the new garments of the righteousness of Christ (Ephesians 4:24, Colossians 3:5-14). The church will once again become a beacon of light to point mankind to the cross of Christ, where grace was poured out for all. In John 8:36, Jesus said *"So if the Son sets you free, you will be free indeed."*

Just as it takes time for the landscape to be fully covered in pure white snow, even so our souls are in a process of purification. Though we stand blameless before God through the blood of Jesus, our souls are still being transformed day by day.

---

[4] *Webster's New Twentieth Century Dictionary* (Unabridged), s.v. "defilement."

19

Clothed in Fine White Linen

Who does not like to look out on a landscape blanketed white with the shimmering freshness of newly-fallen snow? It seems everything is transformed; nature is lifted into an elegance and sense of purity that invites reflection and peace. New snowfall is enchanting.

> *You wake up on a winter morning and pull up the shade, and what lay there the evening before is no longer there--the sodden, gray yard, the dog droppings, the tire tracks in the frozen mud, the broken lawn chair you forgot to take in last fall. All this has disappeared overnight, and what you look out on is not the snow of Narnia but the snow of home, which is no less shimmering and white as it falls. The earth is covered with it, and it is falling still in silence so deep you can hear its silence.*
>
> —Frederick Buechner, *Telling the Truth: The Gospel as Tragedy, Comedy, and Fairy Tale*

If you are near mountains, you can lift your eyes to their summit and, if the air is clear, view the enshrouded peaks so bright you have to shield your eyes from the radiance. The crystalline beauty can cause an onlooker to remain quiet in hushed reflection, serene before the fresh stillness. It seems that pure white linen has been placed on their brows like a new turban.

> *Then I said, "They should also place a clean turban on his head." So they put a clean priestly turban on his head and dressed him in new clothes while the angel of the LORD stood by* (Zechariah 3:5).

Angels brought new clothes that represented Joshua's restoration and purification. They placed a clean turban on his head, restoring him to his office. This was not just any turban, but the priestly turban, with an inscribed golden plate affixes to it, so that upon his forehead were the words "Holy to the LORD."

> *"You shall make a plate of pure gold and engrave on it, like the engraving of a signet, 'Holy to the LORD.' And you shall fasten it on the turban by a cord of blue. It shall be on the front of the turban. It shall be on Aaron's forehead, and Aaron shall bear any guilt from the holy things that the people of Israel consecrate as their holy gifts. It shall regularly be on his forehead, that they may be accepted before the LORD"* (Exodus 28:36-38).

The priests' official role was that of ministering unto the LORD and representing the people before Him. Among the priesthood there was an appointed high priest who would enter the Holy of Holies once a year, on the Day of Atonement. So, as we read about the turban placed upon Joshua's head, we understand the message that God is declaring that *"...Joshua and, by implication, his people with him, are once more accepted in God's presence."*[5]

We too have received a new turban as our minds have been renewed. We have received new garments as we have yielded to a deep and sovereign purification in our hearts. Just like the undisturbed snow-covered mountain tops, a hush and stillness has come upon us; a rest and light burden. The beauty of restoration and the peace that comes with alignment and purity releases a "selah" on our lives. A holy hush has come upon us as heaven has viewed this act of grace for us: the pure, white priestly linens have been placed upon us.

---

[5] David J. Ellis, "Zechariah," in *The International Bible Commentary*, ed. F.F. Bruce (Grand Rapids: Zondervan, 1986), 970.

Jesus invited us to lower our heads and allow Him to give us a new priestly turban; the turban of a high priest, because He is *the* high priest and He gives us all that belongs to Him. He is restoring us to our official spiritual office as those who minister unto the Lord: kings and priests before our God. He is inviting us once again into the Holy of Holies where the blood of the Lamb has been poured upon the altar and atones for our sins and the sins of our people.

This is a day to rest in the work that has been done. It is a day to feel the peace that the purity of grace has brought upon us.

Breathe in the presence and peace of the Lord and let His light burden usher you into His deep rest. As you rest you will be taken even higher. It is in the high places that the new turban is affixed firmly to your head, restoring your position as a priest before the Lord. The floodgates of heaven open to release a heavy rain that pours out to wash you.

Our yielding has brought us into the rest of the Lord, and in that rest He gives us new instructions. We have been prepared through His peace to walk in obedience and authority without the burdens we have carried in the past: burdens of striving and self-effort and failure. The iniquities of the past have been taken away and His light and easy yoke rests upon us, dressed as we are in white linens, wearing the holy turban that marks us belonging as a holy people to God Almighty, possessing the mind of Christ. His gentleness surrounds us and His peace rests on His chosen ones.

Joshua was not actively seeking atonement or restoration, yet God, in His mercy, came and plucked him like a brand out of the fire to save him. His "salvation" came purely by grace alone, and Jesus is still the atonement for our sin and the sins of all mankind, by grace alone.

> *Since you have heard about Jesus and have learned the truth that comes from him, throw off your old sinful nature and your former way of life, which is corrupted by lust and deception. Instead, let the Spirit renew your thoughts and attitudes. Put on your new nature, created to be like God—truly righteous and holy* (Ephesians 4:21-24, NLT).

Grace has come to usher us into a time of renewal. This has set us free from every action, thought, and belief that has been connected to our former ways. We are priests and we minister in the temple of our God. In fact, together we are the temple of our God!

20

You Will See Clearly

One morning I (Kathi) awoke into a vision in which I saw window washers cleaning the dirt off windows on what appeared to be a skyscraper. The Spirit then drew me back from the "building" to reveal that is was, in fact, a massive body with many eyes upon it. The eyes were the "windows" that were being washed. Then I heard the Spirit of the Lord say, *"I am washing the eyes of the body of Christ from all the pollutants of the world that has clouded them from seeing as I see. I have commissioned angels to go to My sons and daughters to wash their eyes so that they will see clearly."*

The blueprint that we have been considering in Zechariah 3 reveals what the Spirit is doing with His yielded ones; there is a continual theme of washing represented in its verses. Joshua the high priest has accusations and iniquities washed away; his garments are changed from filthy to clean, and his behavior—his way of living—is cleansed and aligned so that he might fulfill everything the Lord positioned him for. He needed his eyes opened to the spiritual realities surrounding his situation. Joshua needed to *see* differently so that he could *behave* differently. Jesus told us,

> *"The eye is the lamp of the body. So, if your eye is healthy, your whole body will be full of light, but if your eye is bad, your whole body will be full of darkness. If then the light in you is darkness, how great is the darkness!"* (Matthew 6:22-23).

"If your eye is healthy, your whole body will be full of light...." God is bringing health and purity to the eyes of the body of Christ. With this washing of the eyes there will be a newfound clarity to see as He sees. This washing will allow light into the whole body, causing His church to once again be a light to shine for the entire world to see. We will see physical health come to many in the body of Christ as our eyes become lamps once again. This will release a move of God for physical healing, emotional and mental healing, and profound spiritual healing and release.

The Lord has come to us to wash away all darkness from our eyes. We can also bring our loved ones before His throne of grace and pray, *"Lord, open their eyes that they might see you, the Light of the World, clearly."* Jesus' healing of a blind man in Bethsaida gives us some insight into His work in our day, and how we can pray.

> *And they came to Bethsaida. And some people brought to him a blind man and begged him to touch him. And he took the blind man by the hand and led him out of the village, and when he had spit on his eyes and laid his hands on him, he asked him, "Do you see anything?" And he looked up and said, "I see people, but they look like trees, walking." Then Jesus laid his hands on his eyes again; and he opened his eyes, his sight was restored, and he saw everything clearly* (Mark 8:22-25).

This man had spent his entire adult life begging at the city gates while being ignored, or mocked and spit on. When Jesus led him outside the village, the man most likely expected to be mocked yet again. When he heard the familiar sound of a man spitting, perhaps he felt the weariness of despair, or anger and confusion. But this time was different; the Lord used the very thing that other men had used to shame and humiliate the unfortunate man to instead heal both his eyes and his soul. When he began to see for the first time, light entered through his eyes and lit up his whole body. The darkness from his lack of sight had darkened his entire life, but the when the Light of the World brought light to his eyes, everything changed from darkness to clarity.

It is amazing how God will often use the very troubles that the enemy has meant for our shame to bring healing and a great turnaround. Satan wishes to plague us, but Jesus comes and with His light dispels the darkness. Will you trust God to use whatever He desires to bring healing to your life and light to your eyes? Yield to His hand as He reaches out to touch you.

Lord, I lift my eyes to You, the only one my help comes from. Wash my eyes and restore them to health so that only light is found within me. I also bring my loved ones before You and ask that all blindness and darkness is removed from their eyes so that they will see You clearly. Cause them to yield to Your will and ways. I come into agreement with truth, health, light, and Your perfect love to cover me and the ones I love. Amen.

Confronting A Python Spirit

Recently, I was teaching on the subject of Prophetic Alignment. I shared with the students a story of an experience I had in the nation of Zambia. I was set to preach in the church of my friend, George Palo. During worship, the Lord said the following words to me, "There is a python spirit present." I leaned over to George and shared what the Lord had just revealed to me. George is a man of the Spirit. Immediately he went to the platform and paused worship and began to minister the word. He invited those who felt afflicted by a python spirit to come forward.

What took place in the next few minutes was both very strange and very beautiful. I looked back and some of the people coming forward fell to the ground and began to slither forward like a snake. Others were hissing as they came forward. As the people responded to the invitation under the command of God, George began to cast the python spirit out of people and freedom was released. It was an amazing display of God's power.

After the meeting, I asked George to share what he understood about what had just transpired. He shared with me this is a spirit of control that squeezes life and the will to obey God out of people. It is a constricting presence that results in domination.

Whenever a family, a people group or a nation is undergoing a God-ordained transformation this spirit will attempt to tighten its grip to retain control. The victims will become progressively more desperate to get free, but at some point will become paralyzed under the squeezing influence of this dark spirit. The only hope for freedom is to yield to the freeing presence of God, like I saw taking place in worship that morning in Zambia.

Be wise in how you interpret what is taking place in the world around you. Some people are under the influence of a spirit of control. Do not look at predictable human responses in an attempt to understand how this spirit operates. Some of the victims under its influence look calm like they are in control and at peace, but they are actually being held in a place of control to do the bidding of darkness. They are experiencing a false freedom. Others held in the grip of this spirit are violently responding to the squeezing, causing some to think the visible acts of violence we are seeing are only the result of rebellion and human anger.

You must lay down your own thoughts and opinions and ask God to give you the ears to hear and the eyes to see what is transpiring beneath the surface in the personal life of individuals and the administration of world governments. His revelation will be your assignment to gather wise counsel around you to pray and seek the freedom of those held in bondage to a spirit of control. You can miss what is taking place, even in a place of worship, if you are not listening to the Spirit and you only work from natural indicators. This is not a work of suspicion. It is the result of the revelation of God's heart that has the power to set the captives free.

~Garris Elkins

21

God Reunites what was Divided

Everything starts with God's heart as a Father and His love for us. He wanted to create a family with real children made in His image....The amazing love of God desires not only that we worship Him as His creature, but also that we join together with Him as a family....
(Asher Intrater, *Alignment*)

One morning, Kathi was taken into a vision and saw what looked like a scene from a movie. In this scene a family was together in their home. The husband sat in one room busying himself with hobbies he enjoyed, while his wife was in another room taking care of household chores. As the scene went on she saw them pass one another in a hallway but they did not connect physically, verbally, or emotionally; they merely passed one another as if the other person was not present.

Then she was taken to the rooms of the children. They were sitting alone doing the things that kept them occupied. After that, she saw the whole family at the dinner table. Again, there was little interaction; no holding of hands to pray, no emotional connection, no conversation beyond someone asking another family member to "pass the potatoes." As dinner finished everyone went back to doing their own thing in separate rooms, and the cycle of merely existing in the same house while remaining divided continued.

She was then taken into another vision in the same house, with the same family, but the children were now teens. She saw the same pattern of a family divided and a couple coexisting rather than sharing intimacy together. In this second vision, the oldest daughter approached her parents and said, "Dad and Mom, I see you each day but I can't feel you. You are in the same house but I don't feel you at home. I don't see you connected to each other and that makes me feel divided from you both. We live here but don't love here."

The vision ended, and then Kathi heard the words of Jesus from Matthew 12:25: *"Every kingdom divided against itself is laid waste, and no city or house divided against itself will stand."*

As Kathi sought the Lord regarding specifically what He wanted to say through these visions, He answered by reminding her of another vision she had a year previously. In that vision she saw many clock gears turning over the top of individual lives, families, and churches. These wheels turned independently of each other; they were in close proximity but not joined. The wheels appeared to keep the individuals busy, and each person thought they were being productive, but they were actually just going around in circles rather than progressing. Then God reached down, and like pieces of a puzzle coming together, these individual wheels were connected by His strong hand, causing the "*hands of time*"—like a clock—to begin moving, rather than standing still. Forward motion for the people began as the wheels were brought into unity; connectivity was restored.

God has been touching His divided household to draw them together body, soul, and spirit. He is highlighting relationships and family. This is God's original design for mankind: to be a family. He is connecting His people through humility and genuine compassion one for another in the love of Jesus.

The family in Kathi's vision lived in the same home but they were divided relationally. They were like the separate wheels turning in the earlier vision; close to each other physically, yet not joined as one. This is true of many believers who have lost their *first love* with Jesus. It is easy to lose our connection with Him as we get caught up in the cares of life, and we begin to comfort ourselves with what merely comforts the flesh; causing our relationship with Jesus to deteriorate until it is merely word, not vibrant, living intimacy. It is easy to lose *first love* and begin to move independently, leaving the oneness that Jesus paid such a high price for us to share with Him. God is inviting His bride back into the place where we are "flesh of His flesh and bone of His bone."

He is not only reuniting intimacy and connectivity with Him but also restoring our relationships with one another. He is calling His family back together so that we will not be a house divided. The work He is doing happens in partnership with His Spirit. Where the busyness of life has created divisions and independence from one another, God is calling His family to come back into intimacy and oneness of spirit. He is restoring first love between husbands and wives, and healing family separations: between fathers and sons, mothers and daughters, sisters and brothers.

The Lord is lifting each of us like separate puzzle pieces and connecting us, piece by piece, to create a picture that represents His Kingdom—which is a family. It is like time has stood still due to disunity; like a clock that has stopped ticking. As the interlocking wheels come together, time is reset and forward movement takes place. The Kingdom advances.

> *But I have this [one charge to make] against you: that you have left (abandoned) the love that you had at first [you have deserted Me, your first love]* (Revelation 2:4, AMP).

We must not allow familiarity to cast out first love. Cry out for the wind of the Spirit to blow upon the embers of intimacy and love, first with God and then with one another. We cannot walk in God's statutes apart from love, because love is the foundation of His Kingdom. When we hold to opinions and independence, we begin to create rules and laws rather than a loving family.

> *If I speak in the tongues of men and of angels, but have not love, I am a noisy gong or a clanging cymbal. And if I have prophetic powers, and understand all mysteries and all knowledge, and if I have all faith, so as to remove mountains, but have not love, I am nothing. If I give away all I have, and if I deliver up my body to be burned, but have not love, I gain nothing* (1 Corinthians 13:1-3).

The sound of true family is a sweet sound that draws men toward the love that families share, but things done outside the boundaries of love have a discordant sound like a noisy gong that irritates the hearer and drives people away.

Jesus told us, *"By this everyone will know that you are my disciples, if you love one another"* (John 13:35). If you have experienced a separation within your family or within the family of God, ask Him to bring your "wheels" together so that you will be joined as one. Ask Him to restore your first love so that you can come into a renewed place of intimacy. If you have begun to function out of rules rather than love, you have strayed from the true and pure statutes of God, but He is gracious and eager to restore you in His love. God is looking for His family. He loves us; we are His joy and His inheritance.

22

Rushing Wind

The wind blows where it wishes, and you hear its sound, but you do not know where it comes from or where it goes. So it is with everyone who is born of the Spirit"
(John 3:8).

We wrote in an earlier chapter about the life-changing effect of a song by Keith Green on Kathi's life. He wrote another beautiful song called "Rushing Wind" that had a profound impact on both of us in the early years of our marriage. It is a wonderful prayer given to us by the Holy Spirit.

In the song, he calls out to the "Rushing Wind" of the Holy Spirit to blow through him—through the temple that he has become—blow out the dust and breathe upon him. He surrenders to the work of the Holy Spirit, asking that the Lord would have His way, planting him deep in good soil that his life would manifest the fullness of Christ, and enabling him to follow wherever God would lead him.

This is a powerful way to pray. We desire that the Holy Spirit would daily fill us and guide us and change us into the image of Jesus. He speaks to us often in a "still, small voice" but we must always remember that He is also powerful, and will see to it that the Kingdom is established in our lives and on the earth, as it is in heaven.

Allow the Lord to rush like a mighty wind through you; sing to Him a song of surrender and a prayer of yielding. Your prayer invites the Holy Spirit to blow through you anew, removing the dust of empty promises, past regrets, brokenhearted failure—all the "former things" of your life. His wind blows away the dust that clings to areas deep within us that we weren't even aware of. The Holy Spirit goes to the very roots of wrong beliefs and patterns that you've unknowingly conformed to. He blows His wind of change on your behaviors and old habits. His rushing wind is continuing to breathe upon everything that hinders His people from fully surrendering to Him.

The wind has come, not just to remove iniquities but to realign you in even the most subtle ways. This is why He comes to breathe upon His people. He wants to refresh us and free us to worship and walk with Jesus in spirit and truth.

Several years ago, we received a word that impacted us from a lady we had never met. She told Kathi *"The Lord is about to recalibrate you for the new season that He's moving you into."* She went on to explain that she had moved to a new state where the altitude was higher and the winters colder. After her move, her car was not running well, so she took it to a mechanic, who explained that the vehicle needed to be recalibrated for the new elevation and climate. After they recalibrated her vehicle it ran better than ever because it was now aligned and calibrated to the new surroundings.

We, too, are being recalibrated for new heights and new seasons. The Lord is calling for us to come up higher and this requires fine tuning and adjustments—recalibration—that will align us and give us strength for the future. Asher Intrater writes, "*We recalibrate…by meditation on Scripture, repentance and forgiveness, righteous action, Spirit-led prayer, and by faith in Yeshua's atoning sacrifice.*"[6] This brings us into alignment with the heart and the thoughts of the Lord. Paul tells us in 1 Corinthians 2:16 that "… *we have the mind of*

[6] Asher Intrater, *Alignment* (Frederick, MD: Revive Israel Media, 2017), 27.

Christ"; so we are recalibrated as we know Him and have His mind.[7] The grace and mercy of our loving God has given us the gift of repentance as an invitation into transformation. God never forces us, but graciously invites us to stand before Him so that He might blow on us.

This rushing wind blows on burning coals in your heart that you thought had been extinguished; it is a wind that rekindles the embers, causing them to glow so that you again burn with holy fire, not the fires of accusation and lies that had previously stained us with the soot of shame. We have been given new, white linen garments in place of our former soiled garments. We are clean, re-clothed, recalibrated, refreshed, and aflame with coals of passion and purity, fanned into life by the rushing wind of the Holy Spirit.

[7] Thank you to our friend Daneen Bottler for this insight.

23

Watch as God Vindicates You

As you have pressed in, yielding yourself and experiencing deep waters of your heart with the Lord, you will often experience an increase of demonic weapons formed against you. We do not live in fear or superstition, and our focus in always upon the Lord and His overcoming power, but certainly there are times in our lives where the enemy seems to attack with more than usual ferocity, wielding surprisingly effective weapons against us. But that is not the end of the story because God will vindicate us and bring justice on our behalf!

> *"...no weapon that is fashioned against you shall succeed,*
> *and you shall confute every tongue that rises against you*
> *in judgment.*
> *This is the heritage of the servants of the LORD*
> *and their vindication from me,*
> *declares the LORD"* (Isaiah 54:17).

In the spirit, we hear the clash of weapons being formed, and the mocking of the enemy as he plans how to use these weapons; but louder still, we hear the sound of the wind that accompanies myriads of angels that have been sent out to do battle on our behalf. We listen to the sound of the LORD rising from His throne and baring His arm of justice on behalf of His sons and daughters (see chapters thirteen and fourteen).

The enemy's plans formed against us will suddenly backfire upon him and his cohorts. God will not only vindicate us, but the very areas in our lives that allow "passage" or open doors to demonic attack will be healed and replaced by God's perfect love.

Your yielding invites the fierceness of the LORD's protection, and instills tenacity and strength within you. The enemy will wish that he never touched you!

> *For the LORD will vindicate his people and have compassion on his servants* (Psalm 135:14).

We not only receive God's vindication, but we receive the outpouring of His compassion, which heal us. We may rest in the knowledge that God has not abandoned us, nor has he been unaware of any afflictions sent as weapon against us, attempting to discourage us and dissuade our continued commitment.

Satan seeks to wear down the saints (Daniel 7:25) with discouragement and fear, but we can enter into His peace in the storm, knowing that He will vindicate us and not allow the weapons that have been formed against us to prosper. Instead, *we* will prosper as God turns the tables.

> *Strengthen the weak hands,*
> *and make firm the feeble knees.*
> *Say to those who have an anxious heart,*
> *"Be strong; fear not!*
> *Behold, your God*
> *will come with vengeance,*
> *with the recompense of God.*
> *He will come and save you"* (Isaiah 35:3-4).

Keep your heart pure, rest in His love, yield to His counsel and righteousness, so that you do not align with the weapons that have been formed (as we discussed in section one). As "tongues" (words) have become weapons formed against you, be sure that your words remain pure and undefiled.

It is powerful when we deal with the tongues of demons by releasing the tongues of the Spirit. Many in the body of Christ find themselves praying in heavenly languages more than ever before. There are prayers and intercession being released continually that are in agreement with the intercession of Jesus. This deep and powerful intercession is aiding the angelic armies who have been released to fight on our behalf. The sound of heavenly languages is silencing the tongues of demons and their weapons of warfare. We are more than conquerors through Him who loves us!

Continue to watch and pray and you will see the vindication of the Lord.

24

Stand Firm! Your Victory Comes From the LORD

"Therefore, be very strong to keep and to do all that is written in the Book of the Law of Moses, turning aside from it neither to the right hand nor to the left" (Joshua 23:6).

After Moses died, the LORD instructed Joshua *"Do not turn aside to the right or the left..."* (Joshua 1:7) and then, after Israel had established peace in the Promised Land, and Joshua was old, he gave the younger leaders this same instruction.

The instructions of the Lord will lead us on a **narrow** road, but it is a path that provides great safety for all who travel it. Pleasures and concerns and distractions and discouragements beckon us from the right and the left, tempting us to turn aside from absolute surrender to God's truth, and yet the Lord counsels us to *Be on your guard; stand firm in the faith; be courageous; be strong. Do everything in love* (1 Corinthians 16:13-14).

In the 23rd chapter of the Book of Joshua, God's people are not only exhorted to stand firm, but they are also warned that turning aside from His Word would cause them to be joined to what the Lord had previously defeated on their behalf. Such a posture would disrupt their unity with God, and join them to unrighteousness and compromise, which would have once again brought them harm and captivity.

> *For if you turn back and cling to the remnant of these nations remaining among you and make marriages with them, so that you associate with them and they with you, know for certain that the Lord your God will no longer drive out these nations before you, but they shall be a snare and a trap for you, a whip on your sides and thorns in your eyes, until you perish from off this good ground that the Lord your God has given you* (Joshua 23:12-13).

Throughout history, there have been many sad instances of believers who have wavered to the right or left, causing them to be caught in the traps that the enemy set for them. The beauty of God's wisdom is that as we turn back in repentance, we are placed again on His pathways of truth and blessings. The amazing grace and gift of repentance allows us to move back into victory and begin to reap the rewards of faithful stewardship of the great call upon our lives.

The promises of God are without fail; there are promises of blessings as we walk in His ways and promises of discipline if we violate our covenant with Him. We do not live in slavish fear of failure before the Lord, because in Christ there is no condemnation, but we must also keep in mind God's warnings and sober reminders to stand firm. Joshua told Israel,

> *"...if you transgress the covenant of the Lord your God, which he commanded you, and go and serve other gods and bow down to them. Then the anger of the Lord will be kindled against you, and you shall perish quickly from off the good land that he has given to you"* (Joshua 23:16).

We must heed the whole truth of His Word, not only the parts that comfort our souls. Paul gives us a similar exhortation:

> *Do not be unequally yoked with unbelievers. For what partnership has righteousness with lawlessness? Or what fellowship has light with darkness? What accord has Christ with Belial? Or what portion does a believer share with an unbeliever? What agreement has the temple of God with idols? For we are the temple of the living God; as God said, "I will*

make my dwelling among them and walk among them, and I will be their God, and they shall be my people.

Therefore go out from their midst,
and be separate from them, says the Lord,
and touch no unclean thing;
then I will welcome you,
and I will be a father to you,
and you shall be sons and daughters to me,
says the Lord Almighty."

Since we have these promises, beloved, let us cleanse ourselves from every defilement of body and spirit, bringing holiness to completion in the fear of God... whatever you do, do all to the glory of God
(1 Corinthians 6:14-7:1; 10:31).

So, we see that throughout Scripture, God continually commands us to walk in His good ways, for when we love Jesus, we will obey Him. And the good news is that if a man or woman has wavered and they repent, they are restored. The Spirit of the Lord is setting His people upon the paths of righteousness. He is carefully positioning His people to walk in authority and victory with the King of Glory.

> ***Paul's exhortation to "do all to the glory of God" is more than pious idealism. It is an integral part of the sacred revelation....It opens before us the possibility of making every act of our lives contribute to the glory of God....We must offer all our acts to God and believe that He accepts them....Let us practice the fine art of making every work a priestly ministration. Let us believe that God is in all our simple deeds and learn to find Him there.***
> **—A.W. TOZER, *The Pursuit of God***

As you yield and continue to ask the Lord to do for you what you cannot do in your own strength, He gives you the courage and grace to stand firm and to align your steps with the covenant you were brought into when you gave your life to Christ. The Lord is in our midst, driving out all other gods from among us so that we no longer join ourselves to them. We yield to Him, and in our obedience to His guidance, in the yielding of our lives to Him, He enables us to stand firm!

> *Blessed is the man who remains steadfast under trial, for when he has stood the test he will receive the crown of life, which God has promised to those who love him* (James 1:12).

Standing Firm

(An interview with Steve Trujillo, senior pastor of Father's House City Ministries)

Steve, first of all, I want to talk about the fact that Father's House is, if I'm not mistaken, unique in Portland in that when you began there had not been a church established in the downtown region that survived.

That is true, in the sense that when you study the history of church planting downtown, in that one core, no church had survived more than two years. We were at an opportune time planting the church, to the extent that not only did we survive, but then other church plants survived also. Now church plants actually come in and survive. There was a wall; there was an actual territorial—I don't know if I'd call it a territorial spirit—but there was something in the territory that would kill off the churches. There are other churches downtown that have been there long term, but they quit preaching the gospel eighty, ninety years ago...there is a lot of mixture there. But anyway, the churches that we call evangelical: gospel preaching, gospel-centered churches would either close up, or move out in order to survive.

So, when you started it felt like you were going into a "church graveyard" (laughter). You have told me before that you had to yield to the Lord to even consider starting a church in the first place, no matter where it was, let alone downtown Portland! Then, once you did yield, it was not an overnight success. You had to stand firm.

Oh man! I was a young adult's pastor at my local church: a great church, I loved that church; I wanted to spend my life giving my life to that church and its vision.

So, for the young adult's ministry, we were able to get a building in downtown Portland; a fabulous 10,000-square-foot place that had been a nightclub. It had a coffee-shop, a game room, a commercial kitchen, and this big auditorium where they used to do bands and stuff like that. God's hand was on it, and we thought This is going to be the vehicle to bring city transformation. *We had 175 kids, and we took them to the place and started pressing into prayer, and literally the miraculous starts to happen right away. The very first services—during the middle of the week, work nights—people were coming in and getting saved. It was crazy. God would lead people who did not even know Him to show up at the building; and they would get saved, healed, delivered, and it was just continually like that. And this thing blows up. We went from 175 kids to 650 kids in six months. It became the largest college-kids ministry in the whole state of Oregon.*

So all these things were happening, and while this thing was blowing up really big, we started to get words like "We see this building empty and this movement on the street." And we thought Why would the building be empty?

But several prophetic voices began speaking to me and, without knowing anything, would prophesy me out of the youth ministry and into planting churches. And I'm like: "That's not me; you picked the wrong guy! I'm here the rest of my life." I had been laboring for seven years to see this happen, and now we had a move of God, we had signs and wonders, people packing into this building: it was what everybody in the church traditionally calls "revival."

So I took a team of young adults to Argentina. There was city transformation happening there, and we wanted to get more of the fire of God and bring it back to our city. And while I was there, the Lord told me "I'm going to close that place down. I want a church." And I said "Why would you close what I've worked all my life for?"

He said "I'm going to move in greater power than what you've seen. I'm going to do greater things than what you're experiencing right now. But I need a church to be downtown."

I told the Lord, "You've got the wrong guy. I'm part of a great church and a great team." But He just put it in my spirit that this was what He was saying. And deep in my heart I thought No. You can't kill this!

I came back, and it was going like gangbusters, but suddenly the opposition of the enemy, the warfare, increased. Weird stuff kept happening, and we could just see the momentum start to go. And the

Lord said "I am going to close this."

So I tried to bargain with Him, "I'm going to prove to You that this is worth keeping."

But the Lord said, "You are putting your trust in a building, and I need to take my city. The church needs to be the building going into the city. I need a church that's going to actually live this message, and do what I've asked you to do."

Long story short, the owners of the building changed the lease to be drastically more expensive, and we had to decide whether or not to try to keep the facility. People were experiencing greatly increased levels of spiritual warfare. We could tell the hand of grace had lifted. The Lord kept prompting me: "Son, are you going to do this? Are you going to plant the church I have called you to?" And I'm like "No. No, there's got to be another way."

But by the end of the year, we were down to about 350 kids. We were trying to understand what was happening and what we should do, and we didn't want to give up, but finally I told everyone that we should move the group back into the church across the river. So we did, and then only 90 kids showed up.

My heart was broken. But the Lord kept encouraging me that my season and my time was coming. People would give me prophetic words like "You've been knocked off a horse, but the Lord's giving you a new horse and new armor. The time for the greater thing is coming up, but you need to say 'yes' to God. There is power in the 'yes'."

And I was like "Oh no! I know what the 'yes' is, and I don't want to say 'yes' to that!" So I went through a process...what I was really praying was like Jesus in the garden, saying "There's got to be another way." But I was not ready yet to say "Yet not my will..."

The interesting thing in the process is how gentle the Lord was in wooing me into His will. He wants to partner with us; he doesn't want us to just say "OK, yes, I'll do it!" He wants us to really come to the place where we say "I delight to do Your will."

Finally, my senior pastor invited me to his home one afternoon, and talked to me about what the Lord was saying. I told him I did not want to do it, but he told me "You know; I can see it. You love downtown.

That's where you thrive."

There was such a wrestle inside me that I decided to go on a thirty-day fast, and I realized: at the end of the thirty days, I would know. In the final days of my fast, I was at a revival conference that was being held in the area, and the last morning, the main speaker had led us into this place of being before God, before the throne, laid out in His presence, and I was saying "OK. What do You say?" And He said to me "You know what I'm saying. What do **you** *say?"*

And I said "Yes."

Now at this point, where was your heart? Were you at the point of "Not my will but yours?"

Jesus said "Some things don't come out except by fasting and praying." I think that giving up my dream for the greater dream of God took fasting and praying. It took me to that soft place in my heart where I said I would give it all up. So I said yes, and that very night, a seasoned prophetic intercessor, who knew nothing about me, came up to me and said "Today the Lord has given you a scepter of the city, and He will give you generals to take it." This was in November, and the Lord told me "By next summer, you will be gone." And that is exactly what happened. We started the church.

So, once you had the church established, what was growth like?

We started with twenty-five people, and by the end of the first year, we had more than doubled. We went from twenty-five to sixty-five. By the next year, we had doubled again. Then suddenly, growth stopped.

The downtown Portland "thing" hit.

Yes, it was like the enemy said "That's all you get; now we're going to take you out." We had high-level witches infiltrating us and stirring up trouble, leveling curses against us. We began to have divisions in the church and people started leaving. It was almost like I was experiencing the young adult's situation again: how we dropped from 650 to 90. It was like that again. We dropped from over 100 down to 30 people. At that point we had to say "Did the Lord not call us? Is His word not true?"

When we decided to obey, He gave us so many prophetic words—crazy, off the hook prophetic words—my wife said "This is ridiculous, how many words we are getting about planting this church. How many words do we need? We've already said yes!" But the Lord knew the battle, and He wanted us to trust in His Word.

And so, at that point, I had to yield once again. Would I say 'no' to continuing? I even had people tell me "Nobody would blame you if you said you gave it your shot; you gave it your all. Everyone will support you if you stay or go." So what we were faced with again was "Lord, do I trust in Your word, to push beyond the death, to push beyond the experience?"

My wife and I come from a long line of people who did not give up, so that's what we grew up with. We told each other that God would have to call us to leave planting the church—we couldn't call ourselves. We did not have release, so we determined that no matter how bad it got, we would stay. And that broke something in the heavenlies over the area; and it was after that churches started to survive.

Father's House was not going to give up, period.

Exactly. I remember the day I stood up before what was left of the congregation, and I said "If it's just my wife and I, we'll stay. We will build what God said that He would build."

And so, He did. But it didn't change overnight. There were continual, little breakthroughs, and we remained faithful. It was the favor of the Lord that led us to where we are today. He led me to show up at meetings for the neighborhood association in the city, and just be willing to serve. Our mid-week activities were focused on doing whatever we could to help; especially with the homeless. The Lord helped us have influence and effectiveness to the point that officials in the city began to involve us in solutions for many of the issues the city was facing. What happened was, the favor of the Lord in serving started elevating us, to the point that we have spoken into the lives of major developers in the city; we have spoken into the mayor, and almost every city council member.

See, most pastors in the city go to the officials and say "I'm a pastor; use me." The city officials said, "Here's the thing. You guys always come to us and tell us what you're doing. This guy Trujillo comes to the table to find out what we need." That was the thrust of an article that was written in the Oregonian newspaper. We have worked on every major issue in downtown: from transportation, to housing, to crime, homelessness, sex-trafficking; anything that is a cultural issue, we have been at the table introducing Kingdom concepts and principles that give answers, because the favor is for a purpose. The favor's not for us to be known; the favor is for the Kingdom to come.

We have seen Kingdom transformation in the city all because we said "yes" in the middle of contradiction, "yes" in the middle of suffering, "yes" in the middle of all the wrestle we faced in yielding. The Bible talks in Hebrews on how Jesus was made complete in His obedience in suffering. And our suffering is a lot of letting go of "us"; letting go of what I want.

I've had pastors of large churches in the city come and thank me for paving the way. They laugh, because they think God is amazing, working so much through someone so unknown. The Lord taught us that if you go low, He will take you high.

Our church is not huge; but we had to give up what success looks like to man to go after what success looks like in the Kingdom, to see the Kingdom of God come to the earth.

So—that's our story.

<u>SECTION FOUR</u>

Rejoicing and Walking in the "New"

<u>Zechariah 3:6-7</u> *The angel of the LORD gave this charge to Joshua: "This is what the LORD Almighty says: 'If you will walk in obedience to me and keep my requirements, then you will govern my house and have charge of my courts, and I will give you a place among these standing here.'"*

As we enter the fourth section of *The Yielding*, we rejoice greatly in what God has already done for us. We are experiencing a renewal as He completes the preparation of our lives to walk in greater unity with Him and with one another. We perceive our lives through the righteousness of Christ in a fresh way, for we understand that we have been clothed in Him; and we view our loved ones and neighbors as He sees them, rather than the way the accuser seeks to define them. We have been washed of iniquities and have broken agreement with lies. Now we commit anew to walk in obedience and to keep all of His requirements so that we may be carriers of His authority and may "govern His house" in truth and justice.

This will be a time that authority is reestablished and servant leaders are set in place. No longer will there be an abuse of authority in the Lord's house, but we will lead as He leads—committing to only do what we see the Father doing. We will love as He loves and move as He moves, as an answer to the prayer of Jesus in John 17:20-23:

"My prayer is not for them alone. I pray also for those who will believe in me through their message, that all of them may be one, Father, just as you are in me and I am in you. May they also be in us so that the world may believe that you have sent me. I have given them the glory that you gave me, that they may be one as we are one— I in them and you in me—so that they may be brought to complete unity. Then the world will know that you sent me and have loved them even as you have loved me."

We will be those who answer His heart's desire!

25

It's Time for Abundant Life

I am the door. If anyone enters by Me, he will be saved, and will go in and out and find pasture" (John 10:9).

There is a door—or gate—into new realms that the body of Christ has passed through. As we have passed over this threshold, part of the process has been like receiving a "*biohazard cleansing*".

In the natural, a biohazard cleanup is done to clean, sanitize, and deodorize a site where blood or hazardous waste has been released due to a violent crime or a traumatic event. This is a graphic picture of the kind of disruption and chaos provoked by the thief, who Jesus said is a murderer (John 8:44), and who shows up only to "steal, kill, and destroy" (John 10:10). His chaos and influence on the affairs of this world has left many experiencing a type of spiritual trauma; creating the need for a spiritual "biohazard cleansing."

As you walk through the door of Jesus' invitation, you will receive a deep cleansing from past traumas and hazardous waste that has impacted your life and left toxic residue on your soul. This time of yielding will walk you through the doorway in the heavenly realm that leads to abundant life in Christ. You will not only be healed but you will receive restoration of what was stolen. The presence of Jesus obliterates the work of our enemy, for He tells us, "*I have come that they may have life, and that they may have it more abundantly*" (John 10:10).

The body of Christ has come through many great battles, but we have taken possession of the sword of salvation through Christ's victory, and we go through the door of His faithfulness to possess and occupy the land of promise. After a great battle, even in victory, there is a time that the soldiers need to change their dirty and blood-stained garments, wash themselves, and allow their bodies and minds to be renewed from all that they encountered while on the battlefield.

As we have meditated on Zechariah 3 and the changing of Joshua the high priest's filthy garments, we recognize a parallel picture of this biohazard cleansing that is occurring for us at this time. We are receiving fresh, clean garments and receiving cleansing from everything that has wounded and traumatized us from the wickedness of the thief.

I (Kathi) was taken into a vision of God's people walking through a man dressed in white linens, and as they passed through Him—as if he were a doorway—they were purified, sanctified, and refined like gold. They received the same white linens that he wore in exchange for heavy, war-stained armor, and the bloodied swords in their hands became like bolts of lightning—powerful yet light.

This is happening even now. As the body of Christ has been passing through the doorway of Jesus, we are finding safe pasture and restoration for our souls. There will be more battles ahead and we will fight with the power and authority that God has given His soldiers. We will be clothed in light and purity that is like spiritual camouflage to the demonic forces. The oneness in spirit with Christ Jesus will surround His people with the promised protection we read of in Psalm 91, as it comes upon us in greater measure.

By faith, pass through the door of Jesus. He is clothing us anew with His white garments. He is taking the blood-soaked clothing and the heavy, battered sword from the past season and handing you a sword of light and power for the days ahead. You are clothed in Christ and you will walk in His ways more than you ever imagined as you become more aware of being one in spirit with Him.

This is a good day to be alive and to experience abundant life!

26

He Grants True Wisdom

Wise children heed their parent's instructions. But as any parent knows, it is a daily struggle to teach children to obey, to listen to wise counsel. Proverbs 22:15 tells us *"Folly is bound up in the heart of a child..."* and anyone who has ever tried to get an exhausted three-year-old to go to bed can vouch for that truth. From our earliest moments, we all seem determined to turn aside from the path of wisdom, and figure out our own way.

When I (Jeffrey) was nine years old, I had an experience that demonstrated this. My father had taken my brother and me to a large event in a crowded stadium and when it was over, I needed to use the bathroom. Dad walked to the facilities with me and waited by the exit with my little brother, but when I was finished, I charged out the door and without looking for my father, I turned the wrong direction and was swallowed by the swarm of large adults rushing to get to the parking lot. I was only lost for about ten minutes, but to me—and my father—it felt like hours. Even now, I recall the desperate loneliness and sick panic that flooded me as I frantically searched for my daddy. Finally, in despair, I returned to the seat where I had been sitting before, and in that almost empty colosseum my father found me, ran to me and scooped me up in his arms as both he and I sobbed with relief.

Scripture tells us that all of us *like sheep have gone astray; we have turned—every one—to his own way* (Isaiah 53:6). To go "astray" is to wander from the correct path, to deviate from the right destination, both in the literal and moral sense. While I was astray from my father, heading the direction I *thought* was correct, I was alone and vulnerable to anyone stronger and smarter than me who might have wished me harm. Initially, I thought I was going the right way (it seemed right to me) so I wasn't aware of my error. For a few moments I thought everything was fine. But then, the truth of my situation dawned on me, and I realized I was in trouble. So, I returned to the place I had been with my father, and he found me and ran to me.

Our enemy is a deceiver and liar and accuser, an adulterous and murderous swindler who attempts to seduce us from the protection of obedience to God into paths of our own choosing—which ultimately lead to destruction and death. If we go our own way, just like I did as a nine-year-old, we are sure to go the wrong way.

The ancient Greek dramatist Aeschylus (525 BC—456 BC) wrote *"Obedience is the mother of success and is wedded to safety."* When we were young, if we chose to not obey our parents or guardians, we could be easily misled, deceived, and manipulated. Even as adults, we are not always able to keep ourselves from being coerced and seduced by the enticing and flattering treasures of the world. If we think ourselves wise in our own eyes, we prove that we are foolish. The sheer volume of what we do *not* know is staggering; therefore, it is best to always be humble and teachable, which is a proven path to understanding.

But fortunately, we read in Scripture that in His kindness, our gracious God makes provision for us to understand true wisdom. He has made it available to us at all times, in many ways.

> *Wisdom calls aloud in the streets,*
> *she raises her voice in public squares.*
> *She cries out above the commotion.*
> *At the entrances of the city gates,*
> *she utters her speech...*
> *Behold, I pour out my heart to you.*

> *I will make my words known to you*
> (Proverbs 1:20-21, 23 TLV).

The prophet Isaiah also reveals His gracious heart:

> *I was sought by those who did not ask for Me;*
> *I was found by those who did not seek Me.*
> *I said, "Here I am, here I am,"*
> *To a nation that was not called by My name.*
> *I have stretched out My hands all day long*
> *to a rebellious people....* (Isaiah 65:1-2).

God is always faithful, even when we are unfaithful. He longs that everyone would walk in truth and the counsel of the Holy Spirit, our Comforter who has come to lead us into all truth. He reminds us of the truth today, just as the Lord spoke to Joshua the high priest, *"If you will walk in My ways, and if you will keep My command, then you shall also judge My house, and likewise have charge of My courts...."* (Zechariah 3:7).

God went on to tell Joshua that He was sending forth His Servant the BRANCH, the One who, according to Jeremiah 33:15, brings righteousness and justice upon the earth. As we listen and yield to Him, trusting and following His continual instruction, we will speak and act in true wisdom as we have been taught; we will be one heart with the great Shepherd who loves us and all people, who is making us one as He and the Father are one. We will do only what we see the Lord doing. We will move as He moves and love as He loves.

When Jesus was born, Magi, or "wise men" traveled from the east to Jerusalem to find Him, asking King Herod *"Where is he who has been born king of the Jews? For we saw his star when it rose and have come to worship him"* (Matthew 2:2). We, too, have the opportunity to follow His guidance as we yield and trust Him and wait for His appearing.

Wise men and women still seek Him!

27

Intentional Surrender

One day I (Kathi) was having a conversation with a young man who constantly struggled with a lack of intimacy with God in his daily life. He had been working hard, trying to do everything in his abilities to please God so that he could earn the intimacy he heard other people talk about. During our conversation he asked me, "What does it look like to walk with God? What is my part?"

Before I could form a thought, immediately I received an answer from the Holy Spirit, *"Walking with Me happens when My people yield in intentional surrender: surrendering their strengths and their weaknesses, their successes and their failures, their hopes and their fears. They must surrender trying to earn My love and yield to the grace that I freely offer. For it is yielding to grace that allows My people to walk in My ways and experience abundant life."*

Ultimately, all transformation is a sovereign act of grace that comes by the power of the Spirit, but we have a part within this grace; it is to yield, to surrender willingly and intentionally to Him. God will never violate our free will, therefore our growth and personal transformation comes when we take the posture of Mary, *"Be it unto me according to your word."* That is intentional surrender!

We wonder if Mary felt shocked, confused, unworthy, and weak in the midst of such a high call. It was not only a high call, but it would surely bring accusation and shame to her in the sight of men. Who would believe that a virgin girl could conceive a child? Who would believe that an angel had visited her to announce that she would conceive a child? What would her parents, her neighbors, and most of all, what would Joseph think? For Mary, yielding to God's word was a profound response of intentional surrender.

We, too, must be intentional about our daily surrender. Not surrender that takes the form of works, but a continual yielding to the Lord and posturing of our heart and will, so that we cry out, *"Not my will, but Your will be done in me."* This is surrender that trusts that He would never ask something of us that will intentionally harm us. We trust beyond our capacity to understand what He is asking. We must yield to His will knowing that His ways are higher than ours.

As God's children, we are invited into the deepest intimacy we have ever experienced but it is an invitation that requires a response. God waits patiently for us to reply; He does not withhold His love, and He does not force His will or desires on us. Like the father in the story of the prodigal son, God watches and waits eagerly for our appearance. The moment that you yield to His request, He runs to meet you.

With every invitation from our Father to deeper surrender, our response can be intentional, where we yield in faith to the One who loves us more than we will ever comprehend. The manifestation of Ephesians 3:20—the "more than you can ask or imagine"—is obtained through intentional surrender. It is in that posture that a love beyond anything that we can ask or imagine is experienced.

> *For this reason I bow my knees to the Father of our Lord Jesus Christ, from whom the whole family in heaven and earth is named, that He would grant you, according to the riches of His glory, to be strengthened with might through His Spirit in the inner man, that Christ may dwell in your hearts through faith; that you, being rooted and grounded in love, may be able to comprehend with all the saints what is the width and length and depth and height— to know the love of Christ which passes knowledge; that you may be filled with all the fullness of God. Now to Him who is able to do exceedingly abundantly above all that we ask or think, according to the power that works in us, to Him be glory in the church by Christ Jesus to all generations, forever and ever. Amen.*

(Ephesians 3:14-21, NASB).

We cannot earn this love and this glory; we are not able to accomplish this through striving; it is Jesus who does "exceedingly abundantly above all that we ask or think." Receive by faith the width, length, depth, and height of the love of Christ. This is walking with God and experiencing true intimacy.

28

The Blank Check ("If You...")

In our fellowship in Portland, Oregon (USA), we have been experiencing profound moves of God as He has been creating a deeper expression of true family and beautiful unity, with the generations walking together as one. Fathers and mothers are taking their place in the body to bless and walk with the sons and daughters and the sons and daughters are rising up to honor and walk alongside the fathers and mothers. It is what true family looks like.

Recently, one of the young men in our church family felt led to pray over Kathi, and as he prayed he saw a vision of God handing her a blank check. He said, "The Lord trusts you and is giving you that check to fill in the blank with whatever you wish to ask for." He paused, and the word "WISDOM" came to Kathi's mind. In faith, she pictured writing it upon the check, and as she did, the young man blurted out, "I see the wisdom of Solomon coming upon you!" It was as if the check was cashed immediately. Kathi later realized she was having a 1 Kings 3 moment.

> *At Gibeon the Lord appeared to Solomon during the night in a dream, and God said, "Ask for whatever you want me to give you." Solomon answered, "You have shown great kindness to your servant, my father David, because he was faithful to you and righteous and upright in heart. You have continued this great kindness to him and have given him a son to sit on his throne this very day.*

> *"Now, Lord my God, you have made your servant king in place of my father David. But I am only a little child and do not know how to carry out my duties. Your servant is here among the people you have chosen, a great people, too numerous to count or number. So give your servant a discerning heart to govern your people and to distinguish between right and wrong. For who is able to govern this great people of yours?"* (1 Kings 3:5-9, NLT).

Solomon asked for a discerning heart; he desired wisdom to lead God's people in the way they should go and to distinguish between right and wrong. To have this kind of wisdom is to come into alignment with God's Word and His ways. As soon as Kathi asked for wisdom, she heard a sound in her spirit; a sound of something large shifting. It was like key unlocking a vault door, and the large door swinging open. She was aware that wisdom was the key to walking in the fullness of unity with God in the days to come. The vault of wisdom and favor had been opened.

After Solomon prayed, God responded,

> *The Lord was pleased that Solomon had asked for this. So God said to him, "Since you have asked for this and not for long life or wealth for yourself, nor have asked for the death of your enemies but for discernment in administering justice, I will do what you have asked. I will give you a wise and discerning heart, so that there will never have been anyone like you, nor will there ever be. Moreover, I will give you what you have not asked for—both wealth and honor—so that in your lifetime you will have no equal among kings. And if you walk in obedience to me and keep my decrees and commands as David your father did, I will give you a long life"* (1 Kings 3:10-14, NLT).

God answered Solomon by giving him more than he asked for, and with the answer Solomon received further wisdom. The Lord answered with not only what Solomon asked for, but additionally promised that which he did not ask for: wealth, honor and long life. When we yield to the wisdom of the Lord we receive so much more. God never holds back but always goes above and beyond what we can ask for or even imagine (Ephesians 3:20).

Throughout the Scriptures we see that immediately following a sovereign act of God there will be an invitation for the people to yield their lives. God wants His people to walk in His ways for the sake of remaining in the blessing and breakthrough they received. Zechariah saw that after the LORD clothed Joshua in new garments, He gave him the key instructions—the wisdom—that would secure his future and his blessing, which would in turn be blessing for Israel.

> "*Thus says the LORD of hosts: If you will walk in my ways and keep my charge, then you shall rule my house and have charge of my courts, and I will give you the right of access among those who are standing here*" (Zechariah 3:7).

"If you will…" These are the words of the invitation into intentional surrender to exchange our ways for His ways. This is where we yield our will and once again respond like Mary, *"Be it unto me according to Your word."*

Grace saves us and then invites us into the yielding of our lives in order to walk in the Lord's ways. Salvation happens in a moment, but transformation is a process as we "work out our salvation."

> *Therefore, my beloved, as you have always obeyed, so now, not only as in my presence but much more in my absence, work out your own salvation with fear and trembling, for it is God who works in you, both to will and to work for his good pleasure* (Philippians 2:12-13).

Ask for a wise and discerning heart and as you ask and receive, do not ignore the *"If you…"* that follows. It is what secures your future and releases a greater blessing than you asked for.

The Surprises of Yielding

God called my wife Donna and me, along with our four young children, into missions somewhat late in life. I was then forty-two and though we were believers and churchgoers, we knew little about hearing—and obeying—God's voice. But we came into contact with a young couple who were with Youth With A Mission (YWAM) and who lived by God's specific words to them. For us, this was radical stuff.

Their simple and obedient life of faith began to influence us, to the point where we started to hear God speak to us. And did He speak! We both clearly heard Him tell us to leave our lovely home in Montreal, Canada. I was to resign from my very good job, we were to rent out our house, and leave for missionary training—all within five weeks! Our family, our friends, and our church, though they loved us, thought we were nuts, or at least suffering a mid-life crisis. But we were determined to yield to the Lord's direction. And in five weeks we were gone: with no support, only enough money for one month, and a thirty-day visa for the U.S; but no debt.

We found ourselves in beautiful Hawaii, living in a tent on a mountainside for three months and in a totally pioneering situation. We loved it and we learned lots. Our staff and our base were in a continuous state of shortage of funds, just scraping by, lots of sacrificing and sharing with each other, as in most new ministries. One night a small group of us leaders—in desperation!—believed we were to take up an offering. Half would go to a new ship ministry, the other half to meet base needs.

But our leader, Loren Cunningham, felt that first we were to take an offering among the leaders, believing that we should lead the way; and furthermore he sensed we would come up with 10% of the needs!

We prayed silently, then couples shared with each other the amount they were to give. Amazingly, Donna and I heard the same thing: sell our house in Montreal and give the entire amount—which proved to be $20,000—into the offering. We protested, "But Lord, that was to be our retirement nest egg!" God gave us the grace and we went ahead and sold the house and gave the entire amount. And I'd have to *say, we gave joyfully.*

For many years we simply clung to God for His provision through mostly 'thin' times. He always supplied enough. We had started a new ministry within YWAM: a ministry of encouragement to those who had served in the mission, and gone on to other things. By then we lived in beautiful British Columbia, Canada, and our daughter Laurie was part of our team. We had dreams of a 'House of Peace' hospitality home, but those dreams came crumbling down, and God showed us we were to move from the place we were occupying.

But to where? Our daughter Julie and her husband Vae were also in YWAM with their four children, and were ministering among Canada's First People in the wide prairies, so we went to visit them. At that time our resources were a four-year-old car and some ancient furniture, my small invested pension from my job in Montreal—and not much else.

Then one miserable, rainy day, a contractor and builder of condominiums took us to see one of his creations, which was still partially under construction. Rather than leading us to a modest unit that we had been considering, (one we felt we could perhaps afford), he marched us straight up to one of the best apartments. It had an expansive view of the mighty South Saskatchewan River, which flowed right beneath the windows. The unit had only been framed so far. As the rain dripped all around us, the contractor, Wes, said with great conviction and enthusiasm, "I believe this is to be yours." Then he proceeded to drop the price and we were tempted to just say, "We'll take it!" Even though we sensed the Lord encouraging us, we needed to do a little bean-counting and praying first. We had to make sure we could cover a mortgage if—and it was a big if—some bank would risk giving a mortgage to a missionary couple with no visible means of support.

Upon returning to BC, we started calculating what we might be able to manage for monthly payments. I also contacted a pastor's wife I knew who arranged mortgages for a bank in Medicine Hat, Alberta. Back and forth we went until, to our amazement, she was able to work out a payment schedule that both the bank and Donna and I could live with. Feeling God's pleasure with the arrangement, we put a deposit on the condo.

As the weeks rolled by, we knew we had to come up with a significant down payment to close the deal on our new home. Meanwhile, Donna continued her traveling ministry, teaching in various discipleship schools. In one Chinese school in Los Angeles, Donna was asked about our living conditions. She felt released to share about our upcoming move. Afterwards, the school leader opened things up for the students to donate toward the purchase of our condominium. One couple came to Donna and said the Lord had told them to give $10,000!

Elsewhere, a Japanese friend heard about our impending move and e-mailed to say he had a bank account in the US that he had forgotten about and felt led to give us whatever was in it. It turned out to be several thousand dollars.

One day we received a phone call from a lady we knew from the church we used to attend in Vancouver. She said, "I had a dream the other night that I was to sell off a cabin that I own. I thought Okay, Lord, but what should I do with the money? *The only thing that came to me was a picture of you two in front of me. That's all. So I believe I am to give you the proceeds after I deduct any taxes that might be due."*

We certainly seemed to be on a roll! We didn't ask this lady how much she was talking about, but we assumed it could be a couple thousand dollars, and we were suitably grateful.

Then when we happened to be in California leading a renewal camp just days before our move, we received a phone call from this "dream lady" telling us she had finally freed up the money and was prepared to transfer it to us. How would we like to receive it? We told her that a wire transfer would be best, but she pressed further and said, "Don't you want to know how much it is?"

"Well, yes . . ." I replied hesitantly.

"Two hundred and forty-six thousand dollars!" was her incredible reply.

Whew! Figures flashed through my mind as I tried to calculate what this meant. Added to what we had already been given, I realized we had enough to walk straight into the condominium mortgage-free. We were overcome with gratefulness to God and to everyone else who had made this miracle possible. In the midst of our celebration, we couldn't help thinking back to the time when we didn't even have thirty-five cents to do the laundry. Now we found ourselves in the position of owning a home with no mortgage, and enough left over to buy some new furniture!

These memories came flooding back as we prepared to begin another new chapter in our lives. Our ministry didn't exactly change when we moved to the Prairies. It was simply transplanted to a new location, complete with new friends added to our ever-expanding circle of relationships. From day one in our new home, we felt nothing but welcome—and we were filled with a sense of anticipation about what God would do in the next season of our lives.

We have now lived in this home longer than any other since we were married in 1960. When we yield to God's ways, we find surprises throughout our lives.

~Peter Jordan

29

God Grants the Desires of Your Heart

Trust in the Lord and do good;
dwell in the land and enjoy safe pasture.
Take delight in the Lord, and he will give you the desires of your heart
(Psalm 37:3-4, NLT).

A number of years ago, God spoke to our family about moving from our home, where we had lived many years, and where we had deep family roots, and re-establishing ourselves in a new state. Psalm 37:3-4 was the Scripture passage the Holy Spirit gave us as part of His confirmation.

In some Bible versions verse three is translated, "*...dwell in the land and feed on His faithfulness,*" and this brought us comfort, as well as an exhortation to trust Him for our daily provision. We did not undertake this move because we had received a ministry invitation or job opportunity; we had no offers of jobs or any other type of natural provision; and in fact we were headed for a region where we had no connections or personal relationships. It was completely new ground for us; God seemed to be telling us, as He did Abram, "*Go from your country and your kindred and your father's house to the land that I will show you*" (Genesis 12:1). We were being asked to respond in faith to a request that we did not understand and that made no sense according to what our eyes could see. We were moving away from family, friends, our ministry team; everything familiar to us.

We had done this type of thing in the past, but whenever we did it was in response to an open door; and we always had the sense that we would eventually return to our homeland. This time, we had none of those supports, we only heard God's request, *"Will you move to a land that is not your own?"*

As we put our trust in Him and yielded to His will, we have found ourselves feeding on His faithfulness in the new land that He sent us to. We obeyed His direction, and our always-faithful Lord has continually set a bountiful table of His goodness before us. We have been drawn into safe, green pastures where His love and mercy have poured over us. The move to a new land has become one of the greatest blessings in our lives. He has truly given us more than we could have ever imagined and it has brought us great delight.

For thousands of years, the people of God in every age, in every nation of the world, have discovered that as we yield to what brings His heart delight, He in turn becomes our delight!

> *Commit your way to the Lord;*
> *trust in him and he will do this:*
> *He will make your righteous reward shine like the dawn,*
> *your vindication like the noonday sun*
> (Psalm 37:5-6, NIV).

In our present day, many prophetic voices are releasing words to encourage the body of Christ, telling us God's intention to bring breakthrough to families and businesses and ministries. The posture in this psalm is key to seeing that breakthrough take place. We humble ourselves and commit our ways to the Lord. He alone knows His counsel and plans for us that He has determined and prepared for us from eternity past, that He desires to bring to fruition in the earth so that we can share His blessings and extend the mercies and grace of His kingdom.

We must not commit only a part or a portion of our life; He demands all of it. We are asked to wholly and completely trust Him, holding nothing back; then a dawn of righteous blessing breaks out on our lives and spreads to the darkest regions where people are still held in bondage and fear. The vindication of the Lord radiates on us like the noonday sun, where no shadows or darkness appear. Jesus gave His life as a ransom for us, and He did not hold anything back. In gratitude for the great honor or His invitation, we too offer everything to Him.

God is doing a sovereign work as we yield to Him, giving us undivided hearts.

> *...you are great and do wondrous things;*
> *you alone are God.*
> *Teach me your way, O Lord,*
> *that I may walk in your truth;*
> *unite my heart to fear your name.*
> *I give thanks to you, O Lord my God,*
> *with my whole heart,*
> *and I will glorify your name forever.*
> *For great is your steadfast love toward me;*
> *you have delivered my soul*
> *from the depths of Sheol* (Psalm 86:10-13).

Where the affections of our hearts have been divided and we have struggled with being double-minded, the Holy Spirit is healing us, making us whole so that we might enjoy oneness of spirit with Christ (1 Corinthians 6:17 & John 17:20-23). We are becoming one with Him; as a man and woman become one flesh, in a wonderful and mysterious way we become one with the Lord in spirit.

Once again we are reminded that the white garments and royal turban placed upon Joshua is a beautiful illustration of the purity of heart and renewing of our minds that is taking place as we yield to the work of His Spirit. Our Lord takes us through the doorway of His presence into a spacious place where we feast with Him at His banqueting table.

> *The Lord is my shepherd; I shall not want.*
> *He makes me lie down in green pastures.*
> *He leads me beside still waters.*

He restores my soul.
He leads me in paths of righteousness
for his name's sake.
Even though I walk through the valley of the shadow of death,
I will fear no evil, for you are with me;
your rod and your staff, they comfort me.
You prepare a table before me in the presence of my enemies;
you anoint my head with oil;
my cup overflows.
Surely goodness and mercy shall follow me
all the days of my life,
and I shall dwell in the house of the LORD *forever.*

With great delight I sat in his shadow,
and his fruit was sweet to my taste.
He brought me to the banqueting house,
and his banner over me was love
(Psalm 23; Song of Solomon 2:3-4).

30

Light Shines in the Darkness

The light shines in the darkness, and the darkness has not overcome it (John 1:5).

Light is always noticeable and always draws our attention. Even the smallest flame overcomes thick darkness; one tiny match flickers and suddenly, darkness doesn't seem so intimidating. Jesus came to us as the "Light of the World" and there is no darkness in Him, nor does any darkness affect Him. Psalm 104 begins with these words,

> *O Lord my God, you are very great!*
> *You are clothed with splendor and majesty,*
> *covering yourself with light as with a garment....*
> (verses 1and 2).

When you became a believer this very light came upon you in order to dispel the darkness that had hidden the treasure your Father created you to be. Light is now the garment that you are wrapped in, bringing life, warmth, and liberty.

In the beginning, God spoke and His voice caused light to appear where there had been vast darkness. When you received His gift of salvation, His voice spoke over you and light appeared in the place of the vast darkness of sin and death. *What has happened before will happen again* (see section five).

Each new day the world experiences the rising of the sun. Morning arrives, announcing a new day with the sun shining upon the just and the unjust; all life benefits from its light and warmth. In the same way, each day the Son rises upon your life announcing His new mercies (Lamentations 3:22-23). You are wrapped in the garment of His mercy and faithfulness each day. This garment of light shines upon the just and unjust as you walk throughout the world, dispelling the darkness that has captured and shrouded the hearts of men, women, and children in wickedness and despair.

You may ask, "*What is my purpose here on earth?*" Stop for a moment and consider that every believer wears the light of God, and their mere existence dispels darkness. Your life is created with a call to great purpose; the light that shines from you, no matter how dim you think it is, carries significant impact with every step you take, every breath that you breathe, every word you speak.

> *"You are the light of the world. A city set on a hill cannot be hidden. Nor do people light a lamp and put it under a basket, but on a stand, and it gives light to all in the house. In the same way, let your light shine before others, so that they may see your good works and give glory to your Father who is in heaven"* (Matthew 5:14-16).

We have dear friends whose son suffered from severe physical and mental challenges. In the twenty-nine years that he lived he brought significant light to every person who came in contact with him. He could not speak, walk, or even feed himself, but he could reveal light. His smile and silent love for God and for people shone brighter than that of most "able-bodied" individuals you will ever meet. He couldn't accomplish "ministry" in the way that most people define it, but He radiated Jesus in the most simple and profound ways. His clothing of light could not be hidden.

Whatever season you may be in, whatever you are going through, whether it is a time of glorious rejoicing or painful difficulties, His light shines from you for all to see. What greater purpose can we live for, than to reveal the light that Christ has placed within and around us? He is the Light of the World and no darkness, no pain, and no circumstances can overcome it. You are Jesus' *minister of light* whether you are a mom at home raising small children, the CEO of a large corporation, a pastor with only a handful of parishioners, a faithful and dependable employee, or an evangelist preaching to tens of thousands. No matter the size of your flame, it overcomes the darkness. When you add your light to the millions of other believers in the world, it becomes like the sun in the noon sky and shadows of darkness disappear.

You are given greater authority and responsibility in the Kingdom of God as you respond to His leading and obey Him in the "little things" of your life. By faithfully shining your light in your daily circumstances, you not only reveal the truth and love of God, but you also receive insight into how to minister to the people around you. The Holy Spirit not only displays His glory to others, but He also gives you wisdom and compassion so you understand their needs and how to meet them and give wise counsel. Once again: your life has great purpose, no matter your physical, financial, or social standing.

Yield to the profound truth that your life reveals light. It is time to reject any belief that speaks otherwise. The Spirit of God lives within you and He has clothed you in the light of Christ!

31

A New Script Inscribed on Your Life

For this is the covenant that I will make with the house of Israel after those days, declares the LORD, I will put my law within them, and I will write it on their hearts. And I will be their God, and they shall be my people" (Jeremiah 31:33).

When we were initially writing the daily devotionals for *The Yielding*, we received an account of a vision that God gave an artist from South Africa. It is significant for us as we continue this sovereign journey, moving into the new realms the Lord has for us.

VALLEY OF THE KINGS: A DOORWAY WITH A NEW INSCRIPTION by Lynette Van Todder. (Used with permission.)

First I saw an ancient doorway made of huge yellow blocks of stone (sandstone), the second focus was on the pillars on either side of this doorway which indicated the importance of the building. The color of everything was "botter geel" (butter yellow). The words "botter geel" kept playing around in my mind as if to emphasize that the color was really important. Above the huge entrance was some hieroglyphic writing. As I looked it kept dissolving like sand in an hour glass, revealing a new inscription in ancient writing. This continued to occur as the sand dissolved and fell down to reveal the next writing. I asked the Lord, "What is this I am seeing?" He said, "I am changing the script." After quite some time and after many different inscriptions, it stopped. What appeared was engraved, Greek-like writing, but I could still not make it out. I asked the Lord what the new script revealed because I could not clearly see it. He opened my eyes and it was the same inscription written on the cross above Jesus' head: INRI (King of the Jews).

This vision of God "changing the script" reminded us of a question that the Lord has placed on our hearts for quite some time: ***"Whose narrative are My people listening to?"*** We are to listen to the story that the Father has written for us.

Kathi once had a vision of people reaching into their bodies, into their minds, and into their souls and pulling out books that were marked "fiction." They gathered the books in a pile and had a huge book-burning party. These books represented the false narratives and stories in their lives that they had accepted as truth. Each person's life was divided, like a library, into two sections: "non-fiction" (which was God's Word) and "fiction" (which was the enemy's narrative). Every time a fiction book was pulled from a shelf, a new scroll or script would come down from heaven and replace the book; as the people removed the books from their lives, they became "one spirit with Christ" (see next chapter).

Joshua the high priest stood before the LORD, and Satan stood "at his right hand" with defilement. Joshua had been living according to the narrative of the enemy; causing him to be clothed in garments soiled with iniquities and accusation. But in the great mercy of God, Joshua was "plucked like a brand from the fire" to become a sign and wonder, displaying the incomprehensible grace of God for generations to follow, until the end of time.

While reading our artist friend's vision, Kathi had a similar vision, in which she saw men and women who had an ancient script stenciled on their foreheads. She knew the language was Egyptian and the writing recounted their "former captivity" and told of the gods of Egypt—reminders of old mindsets and beliefs forged during slavery. Suddenly, like writing in sand washed away by the incoming tide, the old inscriptions simply dissolved and disappeared. Just as in Lynette's vision of the doorway, Kathi saw the inscription "INRI" appear on the foreheads of

God's people. They were now marked with the declaration of the cross and their lives were engraved with His signature, "King of the Jews."

The prophets give us insight into the way the Lord is continually at work in the earth through the lives of His people. Isaiah's prophetic proclamation to Israel speaks to us in this season:

> "*Remember not the former things,*
> *nor consider the things of old.*
> *Behold, I am doing a new thing;*
> *now it springs forth, do you not perceive it?*"
> (Isaiah 43:18-19)

The people of God are passing through a "doorway" into a new season, where the King of Glory will be revealed in ways never before witnessed on earth. Above this doorway is the inscription "KING OF KINGS AND LORD OF LORDS." As we pass through we can experience a sovereign work of freedom, as the former things—the old mindsets and wrong alignments of our hearts—are changed and aligned with His rule and the "new thing" He is doing. His rule is not like that of our former tyrannical masters; it is invitation into an intimate relationship that removes all the "former things" that have ruled over our lives and produced strongholds of accusations, burdening us with captivity.

> *O Lord our God,*
> *other lords besides you have ruled over us,*
> *but your name alone we bring to remembrance*
> (Isaiah 26:13).

By faith, we are able to walk through the doorway. The pillars of God's truth and justice are the frame and His name is inscribed upon the doorpost.

You may wish to partake of communion and announce your freedom, for it is your declaration of the grace by which you have been saved. It is agreement with the truth that your life is forever marked by the grace and salvation paid for by the "King of the Jews." You have surrendered your life and you now rule and reign with Him from heavenly places. You are marked as His child and you receive a signet ring that gives you a new level of authority. Your priesthood is restored, your garments have been changed, and the former things, built on the sinking sand of lies and accusation, have passed away. Instead, you are secure upon the Rock of Christ, preserved and defended in His unshakeable Kingdom.

> *Therefore, if anyone is in Christ, he is a new creation. The old has passed away; behold, the new has come....God, being rich in mercy, because of the great love with which he loved us, even when we were dead in our trespasses, made us alive together with Christ—by grace you have been saved—and raised us up with him and seated us with him in the heavenly places in Christ Jesus, so that in the coming ages he might show the immeasurable riches of his grace in kindness toward us in Christ Jesus* (2 Corinthians 5:17; Ephesians 2:4-7).

All things are made new—even you. Speak life, blessings, and truth over your life. Ask God to continue to reveal His story for your life and speak it into every part of your being. Our weapons are mighty for the pulling down of strongholds; so tear down the stronghold of any enemy narrative that still sits on your "shelves" and throw those stories into the fire to be consumed!

32

One Spirit with Christ

"*But he who is joined to the Lord is one spirit with Him*" (I Corinthians 6:17).

What an amazing statement: "...one spirit with Him." This is a powerful truth that many Christians overlook by not realizing its full import. Have you considered the significance, the beautiful reality inherent in these words?

If you read the verses prior to 1 Corinthians 6:17, you will find that Paul compares our union with Christ to intimacy between a man and woman when "the two become one flesh." The apostle warns against immorality and likens it to being joined physically with a harlot, speaking of the joining and "oneness" that occurs.

We have been brought into covenant with God through Jesus' death and resurrection (Hebrews 8:6-13). From a biblical perspective, a covenant is a sacred family bond between persons. The Old Testament clearly portrays *ADONAI* as Israel's Bridegroom (Isaiah 54:5; Hosea 2:16, 19; Jeremiah 3:14); when we grasp this truth, it makes Paul's admonition all the more powerful, because we understand that "*...sin is not just the breaking of a rule or a law, but the betrayal of a relationship.*"[8] The Lord's great heart of love has been broken by the rebellion and sin of His people.

---

[8] Brant Pitre, *Jesus the Bridegroom* (New York: Image, 2014), 13.

But in spite of our waywardness and betrayal, God determined to cut a new covenant with us, based on *His* faithfulness, to betroth us to Himself and cause us to live as His beloved. His plan has always been for people to live in relationship with Him, consenting with willing hearts to His kind and good rule, responding to Him with love, rather than duty.[9] He never gave up (and *will never* give up) on His people, but instead promised great blessings from His marriage to us.

> *"Behold, the days are coming, declares the LORD, when I will make a new covenant with the house of Israel and the house of Judah, not like the covenant that I made with their fathers on the day when I took them by the hand to bring them out of the land of Egypt, my covenant that they broke, though I was their husband, declares the LORD"* (Jeremiah 31:31-31).

> *"And in that day, declares the LORD, you will call me 'My Husband,' and no longer will you call me 'My Baal.' For I will remove the names of the Baals from her mouth, and they shall be remembered by name no more...And I will betroth you to me forever. I will betroth you to me in righteousness and in justice, in steadfast love and in mercy. I will betroth you to me in faithfulness. And you shall know the LORD"* (Hosea 2:16-17, 19-20).

> *Then I saw a new heaven and a new earth, for the first heaven and the first earth had passed away, and the sea was no more. And I saw the holy city, new Jerusalem, coming down out of heaven from God, prepared as a bride adorned for her husband*
> (Revelation 21:1-2).

The entire story of Scripture makes it clear that salvation is more than simply forgiveness of sins—as powerful and magnificent a blessing as that

[9]Donald Wiseman, "Jeremiah," in *The International Bible Commentary*, ed. F.F. Bruce (Grand Rapids: Zondervan, 1986), 784.

is—but salvation offers us much more. We are not invited to simply take advantage of a special "free gift" and then happily go on our way. Our lives here on earth have profound meaning, because from the "*...biblical perspective, salvation is ultimately about* union with God. *The God of Israel is not a distant deity or an impersonal power, but the Bridegroom who want his bride to 'know'* (*Hebrew* yada') *him intimately, in a spiritual marriage that is not only faithful and fruitful, but 'everlasting'* (*Hebrew* 'olam)."[10]

We are invited into genuine relationship with our Creator; a relationship not consisting of creator/creature or master/slave, but a deeply intimate, personal, continuous communion, as He shares His life with us and invites us to increasingly know Him and trust Him. We are welcomed into the wonder of who He is, and we are allowed to fill ourselves as we partake of His inexhaustible love. We are betrothed to the Lord; we have been made temples of the Holy Spirit; therefore we are to walk in purity in both our bodies and our spirits.

As you continue to stand before the Lord, as Joshua the high priest did in Zechariah 3, you are yielding to the work of His Spirit that will remove all places in our bodies and in our spirits that have been defiled or joined to anything that separates us from being "one spirit with the Lord." Your surrender becomes your worship. The consummation that occurs when and man and woman are joined in physical intimacy results in them becoming *one flesh.* Likewise, there is a consummation that occurs when man is joined with Christ in spiritual intimacy that results in them becoming *one spirit.*

> ***...the Holy Spirit...comes not just as a spark thrown from the eternal furnace. He is not resident with us as a splintered-off subsection of God, disengaged and sent down to represent God. He* is *God. The very fullness of the Godhead dwells in Him, and when we open ourselves to the love of Jesus, it is...*our *heart that is searched and explored. We are cleansed and made ready for the consuming fire that cannot be kept a safe distance away.***

---

[10] Pitre, *Jesus the Bridegroom,* 19.

We are prepared for the One whose love must ultimately brand us from within.

—Victoria Brooks, *Ministering to God: The Reach of the Heart*

We are invited into intimacy that defies our comprehension, and enables us to truly lay ourselves before Him as a living sacrifice. Paul encourages us and gives wise counsel as we continue to worship and to yield.

As you come before our merciful God, ask the Spirit to restore the purity in your body and in your spirit. You will be joined in one spirit with the Lord and through this spiritual intimacy you will be offering yourselves as holy and living sacrifice of worship to Him.

> *...I plead with you to give your bodies to God because of all he has done for you. Let them be a living and holy sacrifice—the kind he will find acceptable. This is truly the way to worship him. Don't copy the behavior and customs of this world, but let God transform you into a new person by changing the way you think. Then you will learn to know God's will for you, which is good and pleasing and perfect* (Romans 12:1-2, NLT).

He truly desires us and transforms us, and lavishly pours out wisdom and love. We belong to Him; we are His cherished possession. Incredibly, we are *one* with Him.

<u>SECTION FIVE</u>

Preparing for "Greater Things"

(What Happened Before Will Happen Again!)

<u>Zechariah 3:8-9</u>

"Listen, High Priest Joshua, you and your associates seated before you, who are men symbolic of things to come: I am going to bring my servant, the Branch. See, the stone I have set in front of Joshua! There are seven eyes on that one stone, and I will engrave an inscription on it," says the LORD *Almighty, "and I will remove the sin of this land in a single day."*

In this final section, we remember miracles of the past and look with anticipation to what the Lord has for our future.

We are entering our fifth and final section of eight chapters. In Scripture, the number five can represent "grace" and eight "new beginnings." Our set-apart yielding is a time of grace in which the Lord has graciously renewed and restored us individually and collectively, and is allowing us to shine more brightly with His glory as we burn with the purified oil of our offering. We are being made ready to dwell in eternity with the Light of the World.

We have found that the Lord has made us one spirit with Him in a way we have not known before. We have been drawn by His faithfulness into new awareness of His astonishing love. The eyes of our hearts are filled with light (Ephesians 1:18) and we rejoice in greater faith and authority to bring His righteousness to our lands.

33

He Gives us Pure Oil

The year was 167 BC, and in Palestine Jews suffered intense and bitter persecution by Greek forces sent by the insane and cruel Seleucid king Antiochus IV (Epiphanes). Antiochus had sent troops to sack Jerusalem and butcher its inhabitants, and he instituted dreadful measures to wipe out the worship of the true God. Sabbath-keeping, circumcision, and possession of the Scriptures were forbidden under penalty of death, and pagan sacrifices and prostitution were established in the Temple.

Some twenty miles west of Jerusalem, in Modein, an officer sent by the king gathered the people of the town and ordered them to sacrifice a pig to the Greek gods, since Antiochus had dedicated the Temple to Olympian Zeus, declared Zeus to be *ADONAI*, and demanded all Jews sacrifice to him. Mattathias, a priest and elder of the town, refused to take part in this blasphemy, so a Hellenized Jew stepped forward to do it. Enraged, Mattathias killed him and the Greek official, and then called on everyone who was "zealous for the Law" to join him and his five sons in the surrounding mountains. Thus began a long period of guerilla warfare against the cruel invaders, and the sons of Mattathias and their party became known to the Greeks by the surname "Maccabee"—probably meaning "the hammer" or "the eradicator."[11]

[11] A.F. Walls, "Macabees," in *The New Bible Dictionary*, ed. J.D. Douglas (Grand Rapids: Wm. B. Eerdmans, 1979), 762.

In 164 BC, the small Jewish force, greatly outnumbered, re-conquered Jerusalem. They entered with great rejoicing, but found the Temple defiled and desecrated and turned into a pagan sanctuary. The first thing the Jews attempted was to light a menorah, but could only find one small vial of pure lamp oil. They used this oil to light the lamp, and the story is told that the lamp miraculously burned for eight days, while fresh pure oil was being pressed. The Temple was then purified, and on the 25th of Kislev, it was rededicated. This event is celebrated each year with the festival of Hanukkah, a holiday that is truly a celebration of spiritual victory, of the triumph of light over darkness, of purity over defilement.

The story of the miracle that occurred over 2200 years ago is an illustration of the light that has illuminated our hearts—a light of purity and of the miraculous. We pray as Paul did in Ephesians 1:18 that the eyes of our hearts would be enlightened—"filled with light"—and that we would know the hope of His calling and His glorious inheritance in us: He is creating a holy people who He can dwell with and who love Him and declare His magnificent glory throughout eternity. The light of the gospel, the light of God's wisdom, illuminates our hearts to understand the greatness of His power to us who believe—a power that is like the mighty strength the Lord exercised when He raised Jesus from the dead and seated Him at the right hand of the Father (Ephesians 1:19-20).

This is our Lord's mighty power at work in us; it is a work of grace in our hearts and our lives. We do not earn it. We cannot cause this power to manifest in us through striving and self-effort. We posture ourselves humbly, yielding and trusting that our God is true and faithful. He will fulfill His purposes and promises in our lives. He is the Alpha and Omega, the beginning and end, the initiator and perfecter of our faith (Revelation 1:8, 22:13; Isaiah 44:6; Hebrews 12:2). He began a good work in us in mercy and faithfulness, and He will be faithful to complete it until the day of Christ Jesus (Philippians 1:6). His work unites us with our Bridegroom, creating worship and faithfulness within our hearts, that we would be able to live as the "five wise virgins" with our lamps full of oil (Matthew 25:1-13). As we submit to Him, He fills us with pure oil—the gift of the Holy Spirit. He miraculously keeps the fire of our devotion burning; He is the oil, He has filled the eyes of our hearts with His light, and so we are able to keep watch, longing for His appearing.

The darkness of our present age is no match for the burning devotion, fueled by pure oil, which the Lord Himself is producing in His family. Through the rulers and systems of this world, satan longs to defile the body of Christ, the temple of the Holy Spirit; but just as the Macabees refused idol worship and intimidation, so we too enter the presence of the Lord to worship and to set in right order the vessels of worship: our hearts and the hearts and lives of all those who love Him.

Jesus gives us pure oil that renews and transforms us into a bright and pure light that reveals Him to a darkened world. The disciples in the early church were bright lights displaying salvation by grace to their world steeped in the darkness of deception. In the same way, we are to illuminate our surroundings in these last days.

We need the oil of the Holy Spirit to keep our lights burning in the night season until the return of our Bridegroom. And we have the gracious promise that our Father freely gives us this gift when we ask (Luke 11:9-13). He leads us from glory to glory, and His truth shines ever more brightly in our lives. We are able to release His love and truth to people around us—bringing the light of hope to their darkness—and the children of God will continue to grow in authority and power as we have yielded and find ourselves united in one spirit with the Lord. This displays the true light that lights every man (John 1:9) and will release the power of the Holy One to restore us, our families, and our nations.

34

Lost Things Suddenly Found

Many years ago, we were directors of a house of prayer in Kelowna, British Columbia. During that time, we had many occasions to pray for Israel, and during one season especially we prayed daily for the nation and the Jewish people. A dear friend of Kathi's felt led to send her a necklace fashioned with three symbols: a menorah; the Star of David; and the Christian symbol of a fish—the symbol used by early Christians, which is an acrostic from the Greek words for *Jesus Christ, Son of God, Savior."* It was a special and meaningful gift that she deeply treasured.

A few years later our family returned to live in the United States, and somehow during the move we lost the necklace. We searched diligently but were not able to locate Kathi's lost gift. In the years that followed, we moved to five different homes in two states, but with all the packing and unpacking and rearranging, checking and re-checking possessions and boxes, we never found that necklace.

In early December 2016, as Kathi was putting away some storage boxes, a small item dropped to the floor out of one of them. She was shocked when she bent over and retrieved the charm of her lost necklace. It was no longer attached to the chain, but her lost treasure was restored!

As she stood up, the Holy Spirit said, *"This is a sign for many that things lost will suddenly and miraculously be found."*

These words bring to mind the parables Jesus told in Luke 15 about the lost sheep and lost coin.

> *"What man of you, having a hundred sheep, if he has lost one of them, does not leave the ninety-nine in the open country, and go after the one that is lost, until he finds it? And when he comes home, he calls together his friends and his neighbors, saying to them, 'Rejoice with me, for I have found my sheep that was lost'....Or what woman, having ten silver coins, if she loses one coin, does not light a lamp and sweep the house and seek diligently until she finds it? And when she has found it, she calls together her friends and neighbors, saying, 'Rejoice with me, for I have found the coin that I had lost.' Just so, I tell you, there is joy before the angels of God over one sinner who repents"* (Luke 15:4-10).

These two stories appear in Luke's gospel right before the parable of the prodigal son. Jesus' message is clear: God cares deeply about lost loved ones, and about lost treasures. He heard Kathi's prayer when she asked Him for help finding the necklace, and though we resigned ourselves that it would never be found; suddenly, there it was! Kathi actually found it during our initial writing of the daily devotionals that form the basis for *The Yielding*. His timing is always perfect.

Joshua's story in Zechariah 3 is a beautiful picture of the Lord taking back a life stolen from Him. It was a sovereign and miraculous act that caused Joshua's life to be recovered and restored. Joshua's authority as high priest had been compromised and his call had been questioned, but suddenly the grace and mercy of God abounded to rescue him from the enemy's stronghold and restore all that had been lost due to sin and iniquity.

When Mary responded to the angel of the Lord, *"Be it unto me according to your word,"* that one act of yielding became the doorway for the entrance of our Savior to the earth. As you continue to yield your life and say to the Lord, "Be it unto me..." then you too become a doorway for others to see the Messiah. Your life becomes the womb in which His purposes are conceived.

The recovery of the lost necklace is a sign for us. It is a sign that the lost things and lost loved ones in our lives will be found. We also believe the symbols on this necklace are symbolic of the salvation of the Jewish people; light is coming to reveal that their Messiah has indeed come, and He is *"Jesus Christ, Son of God, Savior."*

Yield your life to the will and word of the Lord as you pray for the lost. Come into agreement with the intercession of Jesus and pray from your position of authority, which comes from your betrothal with Him, for both the prodigal and for those who have never known Him. You will suddenly recover things that were lost and stolen.

Yielding makes room for the sovereignty of God to intervene in impossible situations. It creates a womb for fruitfulness and multiplication. As we yield, His grace restores what has been lost.

35

Miracles that Happened Before Will Happen Again

The children of Israel stood before the waters of the Red Sea, frozen in fear because the mighty army of Egypt, under the command of a vicious and cruel Pharaoh, had pursued them and were about to overtake them, bringing destruction. The LORD told Moses to stretch out his staff over the waters. Moses did and the waters parted, allowing Israel to cross over on dry land. God Himself protected His people; Scripture says He *"looked at the army of the Egyptians through the fire and cloud and caused the army of the Egyptians to panic"* (Exodus 14:24, TLV). Israel was delivered from bondage to what was the strongest nation on earth at that time.

David was a shepherd boy, young, "ruddy and handsome"; a lad who was consigned to the outlying grasslands to oversee his father's sheep. When a fearsome giant named Goliath, champion of the Philistines, challenged Israel and Israel's God to fight, young David took up the challenge. Goliath taunted and mocked him, despising the diminutive youth before him. But David, filled with trust in the Almighty, bellowed in response,

> *"You are coming to me with a sword, a spear, and a javelin, but I am coming to you in the Name of ADONAI-Tzva'ot, God of the armies of Israel, whom you have defied. This very day ADONAI will deliver you*

> *into my hand, and I will strike you down and take your head off.... Then all the earth will know that there is a God in Israel, and so all this assembly will know that ADONAI delivers not with sword and spear—for the battle belongs to ADONAI, and He will give you into our hands"* (1 Samuel 17:45-47, TLV).

Then David, trusting fully in the faithfulness of Israel's God, ran toward his huge opponent and felled him with one smooth stone flung from his sling.

Daniel was a faithful servant of God who dwelt in Babylon, and distinguished himself serving in the courts of various pagan rulers. At one point, various other governors plotted against Daniel, due to their jealousy at his impeccable performance of his official duties, and succeeded in having Daniel sentenced to be thrown into a lion's den. But God preserved Daniel's life, and he was able to stand in the midst of the dangerous beasts, and declare to Darius, the ruler who sentenced him, *"My God sent His angel and shut the lions' mouths, so that they have not hurt me, because I was found innocent before Him...."* (Daniel 6:22).

Esther was a young woman, taken from her people to become one of the wives of Xerxes I, king of the world-dominating Persian Empire. When she learned of a plot to destroy her people that had been hatched by one of the king's high-level officials, she took heed of her uncle Mordecai's counsel when he told her she must do something, because she had risen to her position *"...for such a time as this"* (Esther 4:14). Esther, risking her own life, devised a plan to approach the king and reveal her identity as well as the plot against her people. The king was enraged that one of his own advisors would do such a thing, and had him executed. Esther's bravery saved her life and delivered the lives of all the Jews who had been threatened. To this day, Esther's story is remembered and celebrated each year with the joyous festival of Purim.

Jesus walked among the people of Israel, bringing hope and life, truth and mercy—delivering God's message of light for those who dwelled in darkness. He healed all those with diseases, opened blind eyes, delivered the oppressed from demons, and raised the dead to life.

And, echoing the writer of Hebrews, time would fail us if we were to begin to attempt to describe the many other epic miracles listed in

Scripture. We can also read and hear in the history of the church about the miracles that have followed the prayers and obedience of believing saints for two thousand years since Jesus' death and resurrection.

We know that God is blowing a fresh wind of His Spirit through His people, and there have been promises of a great outpouring as we draw nearer to the time of the end. So we wonder: Will feats of this magnitude happen again?

We have the promise—spoken by Jesus Himself—that we can expect to do even more than the exploits we have known about from the past.

> *"I tell you the truth, whoever believes in me will do the same works I have done, and even greater works, because I am going to be with the Father"* (John 14:22).

The Son of God desires to glorify the Father, and we are His chosen and beloved who desire to respond to His love and glorify Him because He is worthy. The oneness that is created as God's people yield to the desire of the Son is releasing a convergence of the ages. God's faithful remnant has aligned with the works and ways of Jesus, revealed to all mankind as He walked among us.

The Holy Spirit has graciously moved through His people, gently and firmly leading us into lives of submission and dependency. We no longer dwell in the land of shadows, living in partnership with an independent spirit that seeks primarily our own good, that advances our own goals and agendas, that clings to comfort and safety. While He was on earth, Jesus showed us how to live a life fully committed to advancing the kingdom of God. He displayed a life of obedience that fully pleased and glorified the Father; this is the kind of life we were all meant for. He explained this to the rigid religious leaders who accosted Him after He performed the miracle of healing at the pool of Bethesda. When they criticized Him, He responded,

> *"Most assuredly, I say to you, the Son can do nothing of Himself, but what He sees the Father do; for whatever He does, the Son also does in like manner. For the Father loves the Son, and shows Him all things that*

> *He Himself does; and He will show Him greater works than these, that you may marvel"* (John 5:19-20).

So, we are not consumed with false identities we have created for ourselves, keeping to foolish and rigid rules of behavior that we think will make us more acceptable to God. Instead, our Lord calls us out of the religious edifices we have constructed and woos us into deeper communion with Him, creating in our spirits a unity with Jesus that calls out, just as He cried out in Gethsemane, *"...not My will, but Yours, be done"* (Luke 22:42).

From our posture of humility, in oneness with the heart of our King, we have the joy of experiencing miracles once again. Our relationship creates a platform where heaven and earth come into a holy alignment; our agreement with the plans and purposes of God creates a womb where miracles are conceived; they are enabled in us and through us as the fruit of oneness. Just as a husband and wife become one flesh in intimacy, which leads to the miracle of new life, so does new birth spring forth from the union of the bride of Christ as we function in oneness with the desire of our beloved Jesus.

We will see the knowledge of the glory of the LORD cover the earth as water covers the sea. We will be one as His body, in answer to His prayer in John 17. Then the greater works will cascade from God's people; a crystal flow of the living water of His presence, breathtaking in purity and glorifying the Father, the Son, and the Spirit.

36

Do Not Fret...Trust Him

Trust in the LORD *and do good;*
dwell in the land and enjoy safe pasture.
Take delight in the LORD*,*
and he will give you the desires of your heart.
Commit your way to the LORD*;*
trust in him and he will do this:
He will make your righteous reward shine like the dawn,
your vindication like the noonday sun
(Psalm 37:3-6, NIV).

It is a wonderful and exciting moment in a believer's life when he or she realizes that they have learned to truly trust God. Most people spend years suffering unnecessary and unfruitful tension, wrestling with the "fretting unbelief of their hearts" (Francis Frangipane), instead of recognizing the truth that our Lord created us to live in the bounty of His peace. Even though there are often times that we do not understand God's ways; or we find Him leading us in a direction we would not naturally choose; if we rest and trust in Him, He anoints our steps with wisdom and draws us into peace. He becomes the absolute desire of the believer's heart, because in Him there is perfect peace, abundant light, and unfailing love.

Be still before the LORD
and wait patiently for him;

do not fret when people succeed in their ways,
when they carry out their wicked schemes.
Refrain from anger and turn from wrath;
do not fret—it leads only to evil.
For those who are evil will be destroyed,
but those who hope in the LORD
will inherit the land
(Psalm 37:7-9, NIV).

"Do not fret!" If you allow your heart to turn away from trust and mire yourself in the scum and marshes of fretting, it will only lead you away from the Lord's green pastures and still waters, and force you into dark regions where your enemy lurks with traps set to capture and entangle you. Decisions that are made in the grip of worry and fear are reactions to natural circumstances, and they are usually unwise. When trouble and difficulties arise, how much better and more effective is the response of the yielded and trusting heart of a beloved son or daughter who rests securely in the heavenly Father's love and faithfulness.

The salvation of the righteous comes from the LORD;
he is their stronghold in time of trouble.
The LORD helps them and delivers them;
he delivers them from the wicked and saves them,
because they take refuge in him
(Psalm 37:39-40, NIV).

God Himself is our refuge, our strength, and our hope. Proverbs tells us that His name—which entails the manifold characteristics true about Him in His infinite wonder—is a strong tower that we are able to run into and find safety.

God has fully expressed Himself in the person of Jesus, and trusting in His unfailing love will enable us to see the seas before us part; will cause us to experience protection from our enemies; will allow us to bring the love and deliverance of the kingdom to people living in darkness. *What happened before will happen again.*

As we allow the eyes of our hearts to be enlightened (Ephesians 1:18) and we trust fully in the salvation of the Lord, the ragged, filthy garments of fear and fretting will be taken off us, to be replaced by new garments of faith and peace. Yielding to the transformational work of the Holy Spirit ushers in a deep work of grace that purges us of defilement and fear, exchanging it for the purity of righteousness and peace that comes from Christ alone. We are lifted from the miry pit of past iniquities, set firmly on the rock of truth, and given a new song of praise. He transforms the landscape of our lives as our Father covers our nakedness and comforts us, freeing us from shame. He asks only that we quiet ourselves and receive.

> *Come, behold the works of the LORD,*
> *Who has made desolations in the earth.*
> *He makes wars cease to the end of the earth;*
> *He breaks the bow and cuts the spear in two;*
> *He burns the chariot in the fire.*
> *Be still, and know that I am God;*
> *I will be exalted among the nations,*
> *I will be exalted in the earth!* (Psalm 46:8-10).

37

In a Single Day, Everything Can Change

"Listen, High Priest Joshua, you and your associates seated before you, who are men symbolic of things to come: I am going to bring my servant, the Branch. See, the stone I have set in front of Joshua! There are seven eyes on that one stone, and I will engrave an inscription on it," says the LORD Almighty, "and I will remove the sin of this land in a single day" (Zechariah 3:8-9, NLT).

Every one of us, as believers, has a moment in time that the penalty of our sins was removed and we were made new creatures. The day we encountered the love of Jesus is marked by the greatest victory we will ever experience. We were saved by grace and birthed into the endless mercies of being loved as sons and daughters. The timeline of our lives has been marked by salvation's kiss.

In a single day everything can change.

This statement is often used when a great tragedy occurs in a nation, or in the life of an individual. These traumatic moments mark time with a delineation of *before and after*. The tragedy of September 11, 2001 was one of those days in history that marked a nation, as well as the rest of the world, with a before and after time stamp. Natural disasters throughout history, such as the great Lisbon earthquake of 1755 or the terrible Indian Ocean tsunami of 2004, have had a massive impact on the culture and infrastructure of nations.

In a single day everything can change.

Our Lord will also mark times in our lives that suddenly change everything, but when we are submitted to Him, we do not focus on disaster, for Scripture assures us that "*...all things work together for good to those who love God....*" We should reflect and ask: What are the "before and after" stamps on the timelines of our lives? Can we look back and see how those events represent victories? The day of salvation is a mark of sudden victory. Do we walk in faith and expectation that we will see victories so profound that events—and history—change for God's kingdom; or do we more readily embrace the fear and dread of experiencing traumatic loss?

Joshua the High Priest experienced a sudden, single-day change. His encounter shows us the heart of God for His people. Our transcendent Father is truly able to perform miracles that change everything in a day, in a moment. *What has happened before will happen again.* We realize that the Lord Himself has rebuked the accusations of satan against us. Our God answers us, and fights for us, and cleanses us, and delivers us. We can look at the timeline of our lives, and become aware of His kind mercy and His redemptive power that has truly worked for good in our lives. In response to every dark and ugly and destructive circumstance, we can be more than conquerors, and we are able to announce to the enemy—just as Joseph informed his brothers—"You attempted to plan evil against me, but God has meant it for good" (Genesis 50:20). Our Father will accomplish His good purposes in our lives!

As 2017 began, the Holy Spirit spoke to us regarding the truth of Ephesians 3:20: *Now to him who is able to do immeasurably more than all we ask or imagine, according to his power that is at work within us....*

The Holy Spirit directed us to spend the year decreeing and praying this verse over our lives, our family, and our ministry partners. We realized, as we listened through the year, that the Lord was speaking this to many in His body. As the year progressed, God begin to shift lives from the dread of fearful expectations and circumstances, to an expectation of victories and blessings. Many individuals were enabled to shift from a mindset of lack to a mindset of "more than they could ask or imagine."

The demonic realm works tirelessly to convince people of the opposite; to keep them mired in discouragement and unbelief; but as we remain in faith, hope, and trust, we will see victories made manifest in lives, in families, and in nations. As we continue moving forward with renewed minds, continuing in the oneness of spirit with Jesus (1 Corinthians 6:17) we will experience His "more than enough." Our spirits will soar and we will lack no good thing. Though the enemy has come in like a thief and stolen precious things, the Lord will respond with vindication and a greater restoration. We will not lack!

Our God makes it clear that He is able to change circumstances as well as entire societies with a swiftness that will cause us to stand and watch with amazement. We have been privileged to be part of gatherings of prayer that have brought about rapid and profound change in societal awareness and in governmental leadership. When we cry out to the Lord, releasing His heart and praying His will, things change:

> *"Who has heard such a thing?*
> *Who has seen such things?*
> *Shall a land be born in one day?*
> *Shall a nation be brought forth in one moment?*
> *For as soon as Zion was in labor*
> *she brought forth her children.*
> *Shall I bring to the point of birth and not cause to bring forth?"*
> *says the LORD;*
> *"shall I, who cause to bring forth, shut the womb?"*
> *says your God* (Isaiah 66:8-9).

We are entering into a greater grace than any we have known that will usher in victories that mark our lives with good things. We will say "*What the enemy meant for evil, God has caused to work for good. My life was changed in a single day.*"

> *I sought the LORD, and he answered me*
> *and delivered me from all my fears.*
> *Those who look to him are radiant,*
> *and their faces shall never be ashamed.*
> *This poor man cried, and the LORD heard him*

and saved him out of all his troubles.
The angel of the Lord *encamps*
around those who fear him, and delivers them.
Oh, taste and see that the Lord *is good!*
Blessed is the man who takes refuge in him!
Oh, fear the Lord, *you his saints,*
for those who fear him have no lack!
The young lions suffer want and hunger;
but those who seek the Lord *lack no good thing*
(Psalm 34:4-10).

The Other Side of Yes

My wife Jodie and I have been in ministry together in one form or another, since the very first day we met at our Disciple Training School in YWAM (Youth With A Mission) in 1995. We were married two years later and since then God has taken us all over the globe. We have experienced many wonderful 'mountain tops' together and also many valleys. In early 2009 we experienced one of those 'valleys'.

We had really been through one of those very tough times. When I think about that time, I am reminded of my teenage years, growing up in New Zealand, surfing after school, on weekends and every chance I got. Because of the unique geography of the beautiful North Island, where we lived, we had the rare opportunity to be able to drive from the east coast beaches, when the surf was flat, to the notoriously much bigger and 'rougher' surf of the west coast, in only an hour!

I can remember, on many occasions, wiping out on the huge west coast waves and then getting caught 'inside' where the waves were breaking. A massive wave would hit you and hold you under for about as long as you felt like you could take, and then just as you would finally surface, taking a huge gasp of air, another even bigger wave would hit you and again you would be pummeled, tumbling about like you had been thrown in the heavy-duty cycle of your Mum's washing machine. This could go on for eight waves in a row depending on how big the set was that was coming through.

That's exactly what this time in 2009 felt like for us. We had had one hit after another over a six-month period that had left us feeling devastated, disappointed, and disillusioned. I don't want to go into all the gory details, but I do want to paint a bit of a picture of what we were going through, because I know you might just be able to relate.

The short story looks like this. We had suddenly lost Jodie's mum to cancer, and despite praying for her resurrection on two separate occasions, two weeks apart, she wasn't raised. Our dear friend and pastor was also about to die from cancer. We had been betrayed by those close to us and also felt let down by what we thought were very poor leadership decisions by others we were closely involved with.

Another ministry friend had had a massive failure that really knocked the wind out of us and destroyed the momentum and ultimately the ministry, of what we had placed so much time, hope, and energy into. Then we found out that other ministry friends of ours were getting divorced. We also found ourselves caught up in 'behind the curtain' leadership politics that left us feeling discouraged and disappointed.

There were a lot of other things going on, but I think you get the picture: we were left feeling like everything had been smacked out of us. We didn't love God any less and neither did we blame Him for any of it, but we were just so flat, knocked on our butts, and wondering, "If this is really what it's like, is this whole ministry deal even worth it? How can we go on like this?"

It was right at that time that we heard that one of our favourite worship leaders and revivalists, was visiting a church an hour's drive away from us. Despite feeling everything that we were feeling we were still, even if it was a little deeper down than usual, so hungry for God. Something in us just knew that even though in the natural we didn't want to go, that we just had to. So we, along with our eleven-year-old daughter Keely, jumped in the car and headed off to the first night of what was to be three nights of meetings.

We only made it about halfway through the worship on the very first night, when we were overwhelmed by the presence of God. It was so glorious. Holy Spirit started to speak to both Jodie and me at the same time and we knew what we had to do. We both went down the front and threw ourselves on the altar. Praying together we said "YES" to God afresh, a completely unconditional, unqualified, YES! Despite all that we had been through, all the pain, all the betrayal, all the loss and disappointment, right there on the altar, once again we yielded ourselves to God and His plan and purposes for our lives.

That night was a marker nights for us; a massive fork in the road. What was meant to be only three nights turned into two weeks straight. We drove back and forward every night and fully immersed ourselves in the presence of God. We worshipped down in front on the altar every night and experienced wave after wave of His glory and power.

Less than two weeks after those meetings, we had a life-and-

ministry defining encounter with the Lord, (which is an entire chapter and book in itself!). The very short version is that about 12:30 one night, Jodie and I were woken from our sleep by a ten-foot-tall angel standing at the end of our bed. I woke up violently shaking and screaming as the power of God radiated up and down my body, and Jodie hitting me, shouting "Ben! Ben! There's an angel! There's an angel!" It was the angel of Zechariah 4, the Angel of Awakening. The Lord spoke to us that night and commissioned us to 'pour out the oil of His presence and power in the nations.' He told us to start a ministry and call it 'Pour It Out Ministries.'

Immediately following that encounter, EVERYTHING changed. We found ourselves suddenly thrust into an international itinerant ministry. We went from being disillusioned, burnt out, and feeling like quitting, to suddenly being booked up every weekend and travelling all over Australia and in the nations. The Lord opened so many incredible doors for us, so quickly, that we couldn't have possibly opened ourselves. In fact he was VERY strict on us in those days that we weren't allowed to do any promotion or ask for any meetings, or even let someone know we were 'in town.' He wanted to really show us that He was the one who would do it and that it was "not by might, nor by power, but by my Spirit, says the Lord" (which just happens to be from Zechariah 4!) The Lord opened such crazy doors that we found ourselves eating Nando's Chicken and racing go carts with the Revivalist that had been leading the meetings two weeks earlier, and we are friends to this day. That's another whole amazing story in itself.

The bottom line is that we felt we had nothing left in ourselves. Disappointed, disillusioned, busted, disgusted (to use an old preaching phrase); but one simple act of yielding ourselves to the Holy Spirit, and giving Him a completely unconditional and unqualified 'YES' changed our lives completely.

Since then the Lord has taken us all over the world, on five continents in just the past year. We have planted churches, led revival, (known as the Pineapple Revival) that impacted tens of thousands, seen countless saved, healed and delivered, (including almost an entire High School just a few months ago), recorded albums, trained hundreds of ministry students in our Revival School and seen God do the most incredible impossible things.

I want to finish with this: yielding to God is not a onetime deal, but it's a daily thing. In the nearly ten years since this story happened, we have experienced many more 'valley' seasons. Our 'yes' has been tested and has required us to continually offer up our yes to him afresh. My daughter Keely Hughes (who is now twenty) just wrote this in a powerful Facebook article about "Being Faithful with our Yes."

> Keep saying yes to His way, His plan. There is so much power in our yes. When we say yes, we are giving Him permission to move through us, to work on our behalf and place us where He wants to place us. Being faithful with our yes can look like saying yes all over again every morning. It looks like backing that big yes with a million little ones
> —*Keely Hughes*

I encourage you to yield to Him afresh today. You never know what is on the other side of your 'Yes' to God!

~Ben Hughes

38

Beyond Fantasy

You were born into a world that already had been given victory and abundant life before you ever took your first breath. The offer and invitation into forgiveness and full pardon was paid for two thousand years before your existence; before sin or iniquity ever touched your life. Your only requirement was "yielding." His love paid the price for the sin of every man. All debt cancellations have been provided for by the grace that comes from His great love.

The Eternal Son stepped down from His throne to take on flesh and be born in a stable, born in humility, born to be mothered by a young girl whom He created. What kind of love and mercy stoops to allow abandonment to such vulnerability? The young girl Mary believed and trusted the promise given her, abandoning her body to the angel's word, and was honored to carry and birth Messiah. What kind of trust leads to such vulnerability? This beautiful exchange discloses the interaction our great Creator desires with each of us. He has provided for our salvation, that He may dwell with us and reveal Himself to us forever (Revelation 21:3-4; 22:4-5).

Jesus paid our debt of sin with His life, knowing that many would not ever gratefully receive the greatest gift mankind was ever offered. Yet still, He freely provided it for us. He came as an infant and died as a spotless lamb; the perfect sacrifice for the sin of all mankind.

Each day remember and rejoice in Jesus our Savior. The Holy Spirit has given us eyes to see and ears to hear salvation's song. This is the song that heaven sings over the people of earth day and night. Mankind has received the greatest gift the world will ever know. Our debts have already been paid and as we receive that gift our sins are remembered no more! We stand today free from the captivity of sin's slavery and we can walk in the way, the truth, and the life. Like Joshua the high priest, we are *"brands plucked from the fire."* Nothing can separate us from His great love. We repeat it again and again, because it is a story more wonderful than imagination, and it is true!

The fullness of salvation's gift has removed our sin as far as the east is from the west, and we are awakened from the slumber that the enemy sent to keep us from our rightful place of intimacy that leads to authority. Like Sleeping Beauty, we have been kissed by the Prince of Peace and we awaken, rubbing the slumber from our eyes to look into His face. He invites us into betrothal and reveals our royal identity as those who are betrothed to the King of kings, who loves us with a love unchanging and eternal.

King Jesus is your Kinsman-Redeemer and He has moved you into His Kingdom and seated you alongside Him to rule in justice and authority.

> *For he raised us from the dead along with Christ and seated us with him in the heavenly realms because we are united with Christ Jesus* (Ephesians 2:6).

This is such an astonishing honor, we often must wonder if there is some "catch": perhaps there is something we are missing? Are we truly called into a life that is beyond our imagination, into singing a song that has melody and lyrics born in heaven? Can we truly be free to dance with joy, unashamedly twirling with Him, Cinderella in the great ballroom, swept up in the arms of the prince?

Perhaps, even after all that the Lord has done, this still seems a little too good to be true. "Now wait," some will reply, "how can He *really* desire me, and how can I freely respond to Him? I know my ugly secrets, and although He has certainly forgiven and forgotten, I can remember them!"

Are we willing to take courage, because He has promised and He is faithful? Are we able to focus on the romance of surrender and humility? Fables and fairy tales ignite our passion because we recognize, even if it is only for a few moments, our deepest desire for significance, for adventure, for heroism and true love. We dream of the chance to join in the battle for good that overcomes evil, to be caught up in the wonder of being swept away in love, and to have the honor of living a life of sacrifice for a great and noble cause.

It doesn't have to remain a dream. We have been invited into the Story beyond all stories! From endless ages past, our names have been written in the Book of Life belonging to the eternal Lamb who was slain for us. He is the great, noble, and powerful King who woos us by His mercy, delivers us from our selfishness and foolishness, and then catapults us into His Story that catches us off-guard with its intensity and fire. We have been captivated and captured by a magnificent monarch who has determined to use His limitless resources to present to Himself a breathtaking bride, stunning in her beauty, possessing neither spot nor wrinkle, but only transcendent loveliness.

We may feel that our best efforts are just emptiness and ash; but our King gives us "beauty for ashes." So our humanity, even the ash of our vain attempts at nobility, is romantic to Him. We capture His heart in our faltering responses. He has declared to us:

> *...this is the one to whom I will look:*
> *he who is humble and contrite in spirit*
> *and trembles at my word* (Isaiah 66:2).

We tremble with the understanding of His greatness and our unworthiness, yes; we tremble before the Eternal one, the Fire whom we cannot truly comprehend, yes; but we also tremble with lover's passion. He has set our hearts aflame with His burning desire that draws us into intimacy. Just as Jesus—the eternal Son of God—poured His glory into a human container, so He has formed us to be vessels for His presence. We are His sacred ones, formed by His hand. Just as intimacy between a man and a woman produces a new human child, so intimacy with God produces new creation: a holy and glorious people who live to give Him praise.

Our Lord has promised He will set the foundations of our lives with precious stones; He is establishing His glory and beauty as our bedrock.

> ***...the church must embrace her fundamental function: She was brought into being to engage God's heart, not just to meet man's need.***
>
> —VICTORIA BROOKS, *Ministering to God: The Reach of the Heart*

We have been created for significance—for *magnificence*—and our God will settle for nothing less as He moves us forward in our destiny. We are grateful and honored to yield ourselves completely before this King, our Bridegroom. As we continue to do this, He is creating a bride who will, in His power, change the world.

> *...behold, I will set your stones in antimony,*
> *and lay your foundations with sapphires.*
> *I will make your pinnacles of agate,*
> *your gates of crystal,*
> *and all your wall of precious stones*
> (Isaiah 54:11-12).

39

The Fierce Love of Our Bridegroom

In late summer of 2018, members of the body of Christ around the world felt led to undertake a forty-day fast for the final days of the Hebrew year 5778 in order to "finish the year well." There was a sense in the hearts of many leaders that it was a significant time where the Lord's people would cross a threshold, ushering the nations into greater spiritual renewal.

The number forty represents transition or change; the concept of renewal and a new beginning. It is the number of weeks of gestation before the birth of a baby. It represents purification of man and land, and purification from sin. Noah was in the ark forty days and nights while the earth was being "purified" by rain and floods. Forty can represent a new level of wisdom and maturity while being aligned with God's statutes.

As we have gone through this time of yielding, we have learned greater dependence upon our Bridegroom Jesus, and deeper trust in His desire for intimacy with us. He longs for us to go through the door He has opened into His chambers, so we can be with Him and commune with Him. To go through a door you must cross over its threshold; and He longs to lift us in His loving and powerful arms and carry us to the place He has made for us.

Set me as a seal upon your heart,
as a seal upon your arm,
for love is strong as death,

jealousy is fierce as the grave.
Its flashes are flashes of fire,
the very flame of the Lord (Song of Solomon 8:6).

Jesus is jealous for His bride, and His love and longing to carry her and be one with her is fierce and strong. As we yield to His arms, we yield to the fire of His love being lit within us. It is the intense flame of zeal and passion, strong and steady, and it keeps our first love burning.

> ***God has a prophetic pilgrimage for every one of us....At the end of our story, we will come up out of the wilderness....We will be like the bride portrayed in Song of Solomon at the end of her story as one victorious in love, leaning tenaciously upon her Bridegroom King (Song of Solomon 8:5). She had no certainty in her own heart and motives. She trusted only in the Lord.***
> —Mike Bickle, ***After God's Own Heart***

These days of yielding have been a time of being carried into a divine reset and renewal; into the counsel of God that brings order and victory. Yielding to His jealous love for us sets His fire—His glory—aflame within us for the days ahead.

In the days and seasons to come, the body of Christ will come into the "counsel of God" in ever-increasing understanding and power, and the Lord's plans will override the plans of the enemy as well as the plans of leaders and governments on earth that have aligned with demonic agendas. God shares His plans and counsel with those who have fully yielded their lives to Him. We can trust our Father to reveal His "blueprints" and strategic movements that will cause His people to crush the enemy's strongholds in the power of the Spirit.

As we were completing this book, the Lord highlighted portions of Isaiah 8 to us. We read of a scroll where Isaiah was to write *"Maher-shalal-hash-baz,"* which is translated "Hurry to the spoils!" or "He has made haste to the plunder!" We believe that we are entering a time where we will see the Lord plundering the enemy's camp and giving the spoils to those who will steward resources with purity and righteousness. They will not touch what the Lord says, "Do not touch" but they will take the plunder that belongs to the righteous. No longer will we walk in the fear of man but we will walk in the fear of the Lord alone.

> *Do not call conspiracy all that this people calls conspiracy,*
> *and do not fear what they fear, nor be in dread. But the*
> *Lord of hosts, him you shall honor as holy. Let him*
> *be your fear, and let him be your dread* (Isaiah 8:12-13).

The plans and strategies of the enemy will be nullified and the Lord will come in like a flood to raise up His glorious standard against him. Jesus will partner with His bride, who is one with Him and carries His zeal to see His Kingdom come on earth as it is in heaven. His fierce and jealous love will judge that which is unholy in order to plunder what has been captured and held captive by demonic forces.

> *Take counsel together, but it will come to nothing;*
> *speak a word, but it will not stand,*
> *for God is with us* (Isaiah 8:10).

Ask the Holy Spirit to grant you His continual and wonderful grace and wisdom, so that you can walk in love and trust with your Bridegroom every day, yielding to Him so that you may run with endurance and finish well. He is pleased to bring His beloved yielded ones into His chambers. There, where we look into His face and receive His strength, we are taught His ways to grow ever deeper in understanding of His counsel.

> ***Pure love...does not feel the weight of lack of confidence. This is the nature of a bride, because she is a bride, whatever else she is. Love is the bride's single reality and hope. The bride is rich in this; this is what contents the Bridegroom. He seeks nothing else; she has nothing else: this is what it is to be a groom.***
> —Bernard of Clairvaux, *Sermons on the Song of Songs 83*

The purity that has come through the fire of His love has consecrated us to walk in the authority of oneness with Christ. He has given His all to us, and He is our all-in-all.

40

It Is Finished

As we have walked through this time of yielding we have been invited into the finished and complete work of the cross. The Spirit of God has invited us to yield ourselves body, soul, and spirit to come into His finished work. It has been a supernatural work of the Spirit, partnered with our prayers, "Not my will but Your will be done."

What has happened before will happen again. Like Mary, your yielding has brought forth a supernatural conception deep within you by the Spirit of God. It has brought you into a deeper awareness of the betrothal that makes us "one spirit with Christ" (1 Corinthians 6:17). You will find that your life is about to become more fruitful and that you will see multiplication of blessings and of sons and daughters come forth from your spiritual womb.

God gave these instructions to Israel, *"You shall be holy, for I am holy"* (Leviticus 11:44-45; 1 Peter 1:15-16). As you have been yielding to the Lord, He has been drawing you into an encounter of greater purity and intimacy, revealing His goodness to you, and anointing you with the beauty of His holiness.

Yet too often, God's bride has bowed her head in despair rather than lifting her hands in surrender. As she looked upon her human weakness with the eyes of the flesh she could not see what has taken place by the Spirit. She has been clothed in the pure white garments of a virgin bride, made ready for her Bridegroom.

Here is a precious truth: Our Father wants you to be holy even more than you want to be holy. He knew that we were not able to do this therefore He sent His Son to restore us to our original design. This is the truth of the finished work of the cross.

> *Then I will sprinkle clean water on you and you will be clean from all your uncleanness and from all your idols. Moreover I will give you a new heart. I will put a new spirit within you. I will remove the stony heart from your flesh and give you a heart of flesh. I will put My Ruach within you. Then I will cause you to walk in My laws, so you will keep My rulings and do them. Then you will live in the land that I gave to your fathers. You will be My people and I will be your God. So I will save you from all your uncleanness. I will call for the grain and make it plentiful. I will not bring a famine upon you* (Ezekiel 36:25-29 TLV).

The same promise is spoken in Jeremiah 31:32. The cleansing that He has done has been the work of His own hand, by His authority, by His Spirit according to His power and mercy: *I will put My Torah within them. Yes, I will write it on their heart. I will be their God and they will be My people.*

Zechariah 3 leads us to Zechariah 4, where we are ushered into a confident rest by this proclamation: *Not by might, nor by power, but by my Spirit, says the LORD of hosts* (Zechariah 4:6).

It is astonishing to discover that your great and awesome God desires you with such longing in His heart. He desires to fellowship with you, because you are His treasure and you belong to Him. He has called you by name, so that you can become aware of His personal concern and care. He protects and cherishes you as a Bridegroom, ecstatic with love for His bride.

Every unique individual bears an imprint of the Eternal, and He loves the personality and gifts and expressions He has placed within you. Before creation—before anything was—He prepared promises and treasures for you personally, to give Him glory and bring you pleasure and fulfillment.

These gifts, and the close fellowship with your Maker, create who you are and release wonder in the earth. He does not stand in opposition to you because of your weakness; rather, He is for you, and nothing can condemn or stand against you.

As you come to the end of this time of yielding, with the eyes of your heart open and filled with new light, you now see Joshua the high priest no longer condemned, but clothed in purity because the Holy One decreed it.

From now and forevermore, see yourself cleansed and purified and fully clothed in righteousness of your Savior. You are ravished by His love; you are fearfully and wonderfully made; and you are beckoned to continue in the romance of becoming one spirit with Him, joined forever. What God has brought together, let no man separate.

You have yielded to your King and He has been faithful to do for you what you could never do for yourselves. Like Mary, you prayed, ***"Be it unto me according to your word."***

It has been done and it is finished. Our Messiah came and purified your life; created a resting place for Himself. Your light shines brightly—aglow with the light of the Son—for the world to see. We radiate His glory, which is the manifestation of the beauty of His infinitely unique and awe-inspiring beauty. We grow in knowledge of His glory and goodness and we become the evidence and embodiment of the person of Jesus as we yield to the Holy Spirit and His grace.

Now is the time for the glory of the Lord to fill our lives, our homes, and our gatherings so that the fullness of Christ will transform us. We will look at the manifest beauty of His infinite worth revealed to a world that has traded the riches of God's goodness for defiling trinkets, pleasures that have nothing in common with true joy.

You now complete this time of yielding with the knowledge that you have crossed a threshold into a new realm where the shadows of old have passed away and unfiltered light shines like a lamp stand in a darkened world.

Enthroned amid the radiant spheres,
He glory like a garment wears;
To form a robe of light divine,
Ten thousand suns around Him shine....

Raised on devotion's lofty wing,
Do thou, my soul, His glories sing;
And let His praise employ thy tongue,
Till listening worlds shall join the song!
—Thomas Blacklock, *"Come, O My Soul"*

May His peace and joy, and the depth, height, and width of His love rest upon you and your loved ones. The King has received and responded with love, mercy, and glory to your yielding. His glory is key to transformation in our lives and in our world.

We move from glory to glory, until we echo the words our Savior spoke in triumph despite His agonizing pain from the cross; we speak them overwhelmed with joy, overwhelmed with His mercy, overwhelmed by the glory and majesty of His presence: "It is finished!"

Epilogue: Consummation

"I would have all of thee."

Yes. You would have all of me
in fiery love;

You would possess me.
Your candescent beauty would enflame me,
ignite my yielding; my flickering

passion fanned by holy wind
and upward dancing,
met by enkindling mercy:
breath to breath with Desire eternal.

Consumed, I am not destroyed.
Embraced, I long for more,

and I know that You will ravish me;
that I—

astray from beauty's pasture green,
lain thirsty by defiled streams;
dulled to glories yet unseen—

will rest, forever purified, in Thee.

Works Cited

Bernard of Clairvaux. "Sermons on the Song of Songs 83," *The Essential Writings of Christian Mysticism* . Edited by Bernard McGinn. New York: Modern Library Paperback Edition, 2006.

Bickle, Mike. *After God's Own Heart.* Lake Mary, FL: Charisma House, 2004.

Blacklock, Thomas. "Come, O My Soul," *The Christian Book of Mystical Verse.* Edited by A.W. Tozer. Chicago: Moody Publishers, 2016.

Brooks, Victoria. *Ministering to God: The Reach of the Heart.* Cedar Rapids, IA: Arrow Publications, 1995.

Buechner, Frederick. *Telling the Truth: The Gospel as Tragedy, Comedy, and Fairy Tale.* New York: HarperCollins, 1977.

Card, Michael. *Immanuel—Reflections on the Life of Christ.* Nashville: Thomas Nelson Publishers, 1990.

Charnock, Stephen. *The Existence and Attributes of God.* Grand Rapids: Baker Books, 2000.

Donne, John. "Of Christ as Foundation and Cornerstone," in *The Showing Forth of Christ.* Edited by Edwin Fuller. New York: Harper & Row, 1964.

Ellis, David J. "Zechariah," in *The International Bible Commentary.* Edited by F.F. Bruce. Grand Rapids: Zondervan, 1986.

Erre, Mike. *Astonished—Recapturing the Wonder, Awe, and Mystery of Life With God.* Colorado Springs: David C. Cook, 2014.

Finlayson, R. A. *The Cross in the Experience of Our Lord.* Geanies House, Fearn, Scotland: Christian Focus Publications, 2013 reprint.

Intrater, Asher. *Alignment*. Frederick, MD: Revive Israel Media, 2017.

Keller, Geri. *Father—A Look into the Heart of God.* Wilkesboro, NC: MorningStar Publications, 2004.

Manning, Brennan. *All Is Grace*. Colorado Springs: David C. Cook, 2011.

Murray, Andrew. *Humility & Absolute Surrender*. Peabody, MA: Hendrickson Publishers, Inc., 2005.

Nouwen, Henri J.M. *The Return of the Prodigal Son*. New York: Image Books, 1994.

Pitre, Brant. *Jesus the Bridegroom*. New York: Image, 2017.

Spurgeon, Charles. *The Treasury of David, Volume I.* Peabody, MA: Hendrickson Publishers.

Stott, John R.W. *The Cross of Christ*. Downer's Grove, IL: InterVarsity Press, 2006.

Tozer, A. W. *The Knowledge of the Holy*. New York: Harper & Row Jubilee, 1975.

——. *The Pursuit of God*. Harrisburg, PA: Horizon House Publishers, 1976.

Vine, W.E., Merrill F. Unger, and William White, Jr. *An Expository Dictionary of Biblical Words*. Nashville: Thomas Nelson, Inc., 1984.

Walls, A.F. "Macabees," in *The New Bible Dictionary*. Edited by J. D. Douglas. Grand Rapids: Wm. B. Eerdmans, 1979.

Wiseman, Donald. "Jeremiah," in *The International Bible Commentary*. Edited by F.F. Bruce. Grand Rapids: Zondervan, 1986.

Contributor Biographies

Ty and Daneen Bottler are dynamic apostolic and prophetic voices for this generation. Along with their two children Trenton and Kylie, they live in Portland Oregon, where they serve as Associate Senior Leaders of Father's House City Ministries. In addition to pastoring, the Bottlers are gifted musicians with a powerful anointing to release revelation of the majesty and fire of God through their music, drawing His body into profound expressions of worship and love for our great King. Their greatest desire is to see the glory of God displayed through His sons and daughters as they walk in their God-given power and authority. Ty and Daneen have had the privilege of speaking and ministering at various churches, conferences, and schools throughout the United States and Canada, releasing their apostolic and prophetic voices, encouraging unity within the body of Christ and seeing the Kingdom of God extended in authority and power.
(Their website is www.tyanddaneenbottler.com)

Garris Elkins is a spiritual father, mentor, and author. He has written several books on the subjects of prophecy, prayer, leadership, reformation, and life-transition. Garris' ministry, Prophetic Horizons is a ministry of teaching and writing committed to raising up and releasing a prophetic generation to speak to the cultures of our world with the empowered voice of heaven. Garris and his wife, Jan, live in Southern Oregon.
(His website is http://www.prophetichorizons.com)

Ben and Jodie Hughes are the founders of Pour it Out Ministries and have been in ministry together for more than twenty years. Recently they located to the United States from Australia, and along with their adult daughter Keely they travel full-time around the world as revivalists, with an emphasis on releasing and equipping for revival, breakthrough prophetic worship, prophetic ministry, and preaching the gospel with miracles, signs, and wonders following. They are well-known for recently hosting the

Pineapple Revival in Australia which was attended by thousands and initially going non-stop for twenty-two weeks and extending for eighteen months. As well as being full-time itinerant revivalists and prophets, they have pastored and planted several churches, trained hundreds of ministry students, recorded worship albums, and are currently working on several writing projects.
(Their website is http://pouritout.org)

Peter Jordan, along with his wife Donna and their children, moved from Canada to the Pacific and Asia for twelve years, helping to pioneer the Youth With A Mission (YWAM) base in Kona, Hawaii. They served in leadership and directed Discipleship Training Schools in both Kona and Singapore. Peter served as assistant to YWAM's founder, Loren Cunningham, for nine years. In 1988 the Jordans started YWAM Associates International, a ministry of encouragement to the hundreds of thousands of missionaries who have served with YWAM. You can read more about Peter and Donna and their family's adventures in Peter's book *The Last Thing I'd Ever Do.*

Marilyn Ongkili was born in Canada and is married to Alex, a native from Malaysian Borneo. Fourteen years ago, God dramatically called them to sell everything and move with their six-year-old son Jesse from Vancouver, British Columbia to Sabah, Malaysia. Since then, they have been living by faith, shifting back and forth between their two nations, and in recent years traveling to other countries as well, as the Lord continues to open doors for them to serve Him as a family. In 2015 Marilyn's book *2 Hour Dance* was released and has since then been an encouragement to many, through the countless stories of their ordinary family's extraordinary journey of faith. Ultimately their hearts are that both their book and their lives would point people to their awesome, faithful Lord and Savior, Jesus Christ and bring hope and encouragement for their own journey with Him.

Steve Trujillo was born in Cuba to pioneering church planters. When he was nine years old, his entire family was forced to flee to the United States because of intense Communist persecution. Steve and his wife Deborah are the founding pastors and serve as the senior leaders of Father's House City Ministries in Portland, Oregon. They are prophetic visionaries who are aware of God's "big picture" and have been faithful and effective in implementing Spirit-led strategies that have advanced the Kingdom of God in social and governmental spheres in the Pacific Northwest region of the United States. They carry a passion for the presence of God and have given their lives to father and mother people into their God-given call and purpose.

(Learn more at http://www.fathershouseportland.org)

About the Authors

Jeffrey and Kathi Pelton understand our culture's need for encouragement and hope. Through writing and speaking, they escort individuals into awareness of God's profound compassion and mercy that heals brokenness, and they have a unique ability to help anyone seeking pathways into His kind embrace.

For several years, Jeffrey and Kathi led a house of prayer located in Kelowna, British Columbia. They often travel internationally, working with prayer and prophetic movements. When home, they attend Father's House City Ministries in Portland, Oregon.

Jeffrey is a published author and professional book editor. Kathi is an author who began writing for *The Elijah List* publication over a decade ago. She continues to write articles for *The Elijah List* and other prophetic newsletters, has written a devotional book, and contributes to various blogs that she and Jeffrey maintain. Together, they seek to advance the Kingdom of God as they release prophetic encouragement and clear biblical teaching through Inscribe Ministries, and in leadership in their local congregation.

Jeffrey and Kathi live in Tigard, Oregon and have four adult children and three grandchildren.

28677654R00133

Made in the USA
Lexington, KY
18 January 2019